The Sons of of Cannibals

and more tales from Vanuatu

Bryan Webb

ISBN: 0986271403
ISBN 13: 9780986271403

By Bryan Webb

Hungry Devils and Other Tales from Vanuatu

Spend and Be Spent

To Renee

My everything.

Table of Contents

Preface

Vanuatu, the setting for these stories, has been my home for the last sixteen years. This tiny Y-shaped archipelago of sixty-five islands, one hundred plus languages, and thousands of tiny villages captured my heart the first time I visited and holds it still.

The collection of stories that follows consists of my best efforts to present a frank view of life in Vanuatu. There are cameos of some of my favorite people, like George. You will find descriptions of some of my favorite places, like Vinmavis. You are welcome to laugh at my foibles in "Driving Lessons."

Telling some of these stories makes me uncomfortable; "In Conclusion" recounts one of my many failures, "When the Roof Rots" takes a look at some of the things I and others have done wrong in missions, and "Hokua Means Wind" brings back memories of a narrow escape on stormy seas.

I have tried to deal with some of the issues that weigh on me as an eighteen-year veteran of world missions. "What if?" explores the motives, both right and wrong, in missions. "A Misunderstood Kindness" addresses the pitfalls of unexamined expressions of compassion. "Pastor Joe" deals with the unfortunate consequences of good intentions gone awry.

Finally there are stories of hope and redemption: "The New Sam," "McKenzie's Candle," and of course "The Sons of Cannibals," an amazing story that displays the power of God's redeeming love.

As you immerse yourself in these stories, I hope that Vanuatu will come alive for you, that for just a moment, you will glimpse this wonderful place I call home. I hope you will share my journey of tears, laughter, and rejoicing. I pray the Holy Spirit will use these simple words to propel you to your greatest efforts yet in missions so that all may hear.

Bryan

A Moonlit Walk

Few things inspire romantic thoughts like a moonlit walk. Boring, drab, and even dirty environments are transformed by a pale moon bathing the world in silver light. There are no colors in moonlight. There are mysterious black shadows, gray borders to the inky darkness, vague, half-lit, enchanting arbors beneath wispy fronds, thin, lustrous threads along exposed edges, and broad, gleaming, silvery pathways. Moonlight coats the world like a fresh blanket of snow, transforming the mundane places of our lives into a charming, alluring wonderland.

If moonlight on the commonplace brings out the hidden poet, imagine its effect on the spectacular. Lovers dream of the Eiffel Tower awash in moonlight or a dancing silver path reflecting off the canals of Venice. Imagine walking a moonlit beach: broad low-hung trees creating mysterious shadows, tall coconut palms with lacy fronds throwing long, soft silhouettes across silvery-white sand, the moon path gleaming across the bay, dancing with each wave, winking at you from the top of each ripple.

I confess that when I think of moonlit walks, I imagine a seaside stroll with Renee. I imagine the tender clasp of our hands, the softness of her fingers wrapped around mine. I envision her delicate silhouette softened by shadow and outlined with lustrous light. I conjure the scent of her perfume and the soft caress of her silken hair brushing against my cheek. Thinking of moonlit walks, I never imagined holding the calloused hand of a half-naked man while walking down a jungle path. Yet that's exactly where I am tonight.

I have returned to the island of Pentecost after a three-year absence. I want to visit Pastor Stewart, who assisted me so much on my last trip here. I want to return to Ponmil and other villages where I worked with a team from Health Care Ministries to present Christ to the Sa tribe. I want to hike to Bonlap and meet with the new chief there. I have come to prepare the way for a second medical team to come to Pentecost, part of a multiyear strategy to see churches established in the unreached villages of the Sa.

The trip from Espiritu Santo to Pentecost is a short plane ride. The Twin Otter plane barely reaches altitude before beginning its descent to the bare asphalt runway at Lonorore. Pastor Stewart meets Pastor Peter Solomon and me as we step across the narrow tarmac. He grabs my backpack and explains that the road has washed out, so we will have to hike a little. He leads us through a gap in the airport fence, across the runway, through a thicket of *burao* trees, and over a log that has fallen across a small creek and onto a pebble beach.

A small, yellow fiberglass boat bobs in the surf just off the beach. We wade out to the boat, stow our bags in the sheltered bow, and begin to trace the coast of South Pentecost. As we visit, I am entranced by the natural beauty of Pentecost. The ocean shades from translucent greens and blues to stunning aquas and breathtaking indigo moving from the shore to the impossibly calm water beneath our boat.

We go ashore at the famously beautiful pebble beach at Ranputor. A worn Toyota Land Cruiser waits for us there. We toss our bags into the back, and I claim the sole inside passenger seat; I have made the trip enough times to value a seat belt. The truck begins the climb from the beach to the spine of mountains that run the length of Pentecost. The tires spin and spit gravel as we round hairpin curves, climb unthinkable grades, and dance along the edges of sheer drop-offs. High in the mountains, the road straddles a narrow ridge. A cluster of houses spills off the hillside to the south. We have reached Ponmil.

Tonight Pastor Peter and I will conduct the first of several services during our visit. Typical of most Ni-Vanuatu villages, Ponmil is virtually abandoned in the day. A few old folks and babies greet us. "Don't worry, missionary," they tell me. "Everyone knows you are coming. They will be here tonight." Pastor Peter and I find a place for our sleeping mats and wait for darkness.

As the sun sets, we settle into the small covered porch of the only store. Pastor Peter begins strumming on his guitar and singing Bislama choruses. Further down in the village, I hear the rhythmic *thump, thump* of men beating out kava and wonder how many will attend. I needn't worry. Not only was is there a good showing from Ponmil, but Chief Wabak and most of the village of Lonlipli make the two-hour climb to be in the service.

Chief Wabak's entourage is dressed in the traditional custom manner of Pentecost, consisting of nothing but a *nambas* (a small penis wrap) for the men and grass skirts for the women. I am thrilled to see that he and a number of leading men from his community are present. Only three years ago, they had been very reluctant to allow me to share the gospel in Lonlipli. Today they have made a long hike to be in a church service. What a fantastic change!

Following the service, Chief Wabak and his men crowd around me, asking questions about my family and the doctors who had accompanied me on my last visit. Together we look at pictures of America, and I tell story after story of the two years I spent in the States.

Around eleven o'clock, the conversation dies down. I am out of stories, and they seem to be out of questions, yet no one seems ready to move. I look out over the moonlit village and wonder when, if ever, the evening will end. I am thrilled to see them but baffled by how late they are staying.

"Will you be sleeping here tonight?" I ask.

"No," Chief Wabak answers without any further explanation. In my mind's eye, I trace the path down the side of the mountain and into the valley where Lonlipli is located. The path is not too treacherous, but I still wouldn't want to walk it in the dark.

During a break in the conversation, I look at Pastor Peter with the question in my eyes: "What are they waiting for?"

"Missionary," he whispers, "they haven't seen you in so long they are finding it difficult to leave you. They don't want to be the ones to leave."

I look at Chief Wabak, his wife and small children. I know they are tired. I know it is a long way home. I know I will not be passing this way again soon. I understand their reluctance to go. How can I help?

I stand and take the chief's calloused hand in mine. *"Ale jif, bae yumi jes wokbaot tugeta.* Come Chief, lets walk together." Hand in hand, we step out into the moonlit path. Behind us I can hear his men and family following. I look back and see most of the village of Lonlipli strung out behind us. "Oh, Jesus," I pray under my breath, "if only I can get them to follow you like this."

I pray for the day that Chief Wabak will put his hand in the hand of the Master and the two of them lead the people of Lonlipli on the path of life.

The Power of Presence

And how can they preach unless they are sent? —Romans 10:15a

White Grass is a beautiful little alpine village. It sits on the crest of a mountain overlooking the Jordan River valley. On clear days, you can see where the Ora and Lape Rivers join together to form the Jordan. The Jordan River weaves back and forth like a braided rope. A glistening ribbon of sparkling water courses over an ash-gray riverbed that cuts its way through some of the thickest rainforest on earth to reach the immense stretch of blue called Big Bay.

On cloudy days, White Grass is an island to itself: a patch of green grass crisscrossed with muddy paths and ringed by quaint thatch huts and fringed with feathery palm fronds. In the rainy season, springs seem to burst from every crevice, and the whole mountainside is a symphony of gurgling streams and miniature waterfalls.

Just to the east of White Grass, a small river drops off the mountainside into the valley below. It does so in a series of small waterfalls and clear, calm pools. It is the perfect place to take the family swimming.

I took a day off in Vanuatu. I took my wife and kids three hours out of town on roads that you would not recognize as roads. We made our way through the rugged mountains in the interior of Santo, over the Lape and Ora Rivers. In front of an astonished group of onlookers in the village of Ankuru, I slipped the truck into four-wheel drive and, with thick knobby tires slipping and sliding, climbed up the final mountain to the village of White Grass.

I pulled into the open space before Chief Norman's *nakamal*. The noise of the truck's arrival drew nearly the full village out of their huts and gardens. (Trucks are not a common occurrence in White Grass, because the road is so bad. Once every week or so, a brave transport driver will make the daring trip from Ankuru, over the mountains and down to the coast at Malao.) I introduced Renee and the kids to the villagers and, after a time of polite conversation, asked Chief Norman if we could swim in their river. He heartily agreed and invited us to lunch after we finished with our swim.

When I purchased my truck, I received a single key. I was told that a spare key would be in the mail. Naïvely, I believed them. It was a full six years before I would receive a second key. The key to my truck was joined to the key ring with a small bit of plastic. The plastic on my key had broken. What I had for my truck was a single loose key. Since the kids and I would be swimming, I gave the key to Renee. It was a good plan.

We had not swum long when the kids asked to move up the river to the next waterfall. Bryan and Alecia darted ahead, eager to be the first to jump in the pool beneath the fall. I was completely focused on Drew, who toddled along the riverbank with uneven steps. Renee came behind holding the key. I heard a gasp and looked back to see her slipping on a rock and sitting down hard in the river. Her hands were empty. The key was gone.

Later that afternoon, we trudged our way up the small hill from the river into the village proper. I knew I had to tell the chief what had happened as we would most likely be his uninvited guests for the next week while we waited for the next truck to pass through. In the *nakamal*, we sat with the chief and his wife and ate a simple lunch of boiled taro. "Chief, I have a problem," I told him. "My wife dropped my key in the river."

"No problem," he replied. "I have a young man here who has diving glasses. He will find your key."

I have to admit that I was less than optimistic that the young man could find my key in a waterfall. However, in less than an hour, he returned, proudly displaying my key. I slapped him on the back, praising what a good diver he was and thanking him profusely. I sat in my truck, slipped the key into the ignition, and started the truck. Chief Norman reached through the open window and laid his hand on my arm. "Missionary, I need to talk with you." I thought, "Just how much will I have to pay for this key!"

Chief Norman led me to a bamboo bench at the side of the village. To my right was a primitive bamboo aqueduct that brought spring water into the village from a spring above the waterfalls. Large stones had been set beneath the stream so that villagers could collect their water or bathe without sinking into mud. As we sat, a well-built pygmy man clad only in a loincloth stepped onto the stones beneath the aqueduct. He carefully sipped from the smooth stream of cool water and then stepped under the stream for an impromptu shower. He removed himself from the stream, shook himself dry, and sauntered over to join us. Soon a half circle of village men surrounded us. Most were dressed in only a loincloth, though Chief Norman was wearing a tattered T-shirt and well-worn shorts.

The chief started our conversation with a series of questions. I answered patiently, sure that eventually we would come around to the matter of compensation to the young diver. "Missionary, your wife lost your key?"

"Yes," I answered.

"Missionary, you didn't beat her?"

"No, I don't beat my wife."

"Yes, I thought so, missionary, but you didn't even swear at her!"

"No, Chief, I don't swear, but even if I did, I can't see how it would have helped to find the key."

What the chief said next startled me: "Missionary, if it were me or one of my men here"—he gestured to the circle of men surrounding us—"we would have beaten our wives. I think you should stay here a little while and talk to us about marriage." What started as a day off opened into an amazing opportunity to share the life-transforming effect of the gospel in a community where the villagers still practiced the custom religion of their ancestors.

The issue here is presence. That is what Paul is driving at in Romans 10:15a (ESV): "How can they preach unless they are sent?" Someone has to go; someone has to be present. Some modern theories of missions resist sending a traditional missionary. They point to the high cost of a Western missionary and insist that whatever work the missionary might accomplish could be done by a hired local at significant savings. Their focus is wrong. Missions has never been about task. Missions is about presence.

Presence is not about getting a job done. Presence is who you are as you accomplish the task. Traditional missionaries are chosen on the basis that their supporting churches know them. Their churches have been able to witness their lives over an extended period of time and believe that their lives will represent Christ to those to whom they are sent. Never underestimate the effect of a consistent Christian life.

Half of all the people in the world that do not have a personal relationship with Christ today live in a community where there are no Christians. Someone needs to be present.

Driving Lessons

The truck weaved right and left across the narrow gravel road in a desperate attempt to dodge potholes and ruts, bouncing violently up and down as it careened over the uneven surface. Gravel popped and sprayed from the thickly treaded tires with each maneuver as the truck continued to accelerate as it plunged down the steep mountainside. On the right side, the rock face was thickly covered, carpeted with moss and vines. To the left, the ground dropped away in a dizzying free fall to the riverbed below. I clung to the steering wheel, stood on the brakes, and pleaded with God to get me safely to the bottom of this mountain. I had never dreamed it was possible to drive over such terrain. Welcome to Big Bay, Santo.

Even in my panicked state, I tried desperately to maintain a game face. In the passenger seat was Chief Norman. I could imagine far too easily the thoughts flying through his mind. Still, he too had a game face on. We shouted to be heard over the roar of the road and smiled and laughed like a couple of idiots, though I am sure we both anticipated a violent departure from the road. Finally we came to the bottom of the grade. I shifted to first in the narrow flat curve of road connecting two mountains and began the ascent of the next. I was relieved to have completed the descent but was dreading the climb ahead of me.

In the quiet of the moment, Chief Norman congratulated me on my driving skill. "I'm glad you're not like other white men," he said. "Other white men would wait till the truck had accelerated beyond their control before trying to downshift. You knew to downshift before you had to." I looked at him quizzically. Downshift? I hadn't downshifted. Did he think I had downshifted?

I questioned him: "What was that?"

"Well," he answered, "many truck drivers wouldn't know to downshift before starting a steep grade. They would leave the truck in four-wheel-drive high. They would try to take the trip down in fourth or fifth gear. I'm just glad you are a better driver than that; otherwise it could have gotten bad back there." I was puzzled. Didn't he realize I had just made the mistakes he described?

In my defense, I am from Texas. Our roads are paved, and we don't have much in the way of hills, much less mountains. Nothing in my past driving experience had prepared me for what I faced on the mission field. But Chief Norman did more than give me a driving lesson that day; he taught me a lesson in indirect communication.

Americans like direct communication. We lose patience when people beat around the bush; we want them to get to the point. We insist that others lay all their cards on the table. We like to get things off our chest. We want people to say what they mean and mean what they say.

Our objective in communication is clarity. In our quest for clarity, we are happy to tell it like it is and let the chips fall where they may. Sometimes we insist that the truth hurts, yet honesty is still the best policy. If clarity requires a breach in relationship, we consider that acceptable collateral damage.

This is not to say all Americans are rude. We value tact; some men are more diplomatic than others, and most women speak more indirectly than most men in an effort to avoid offending others. Still, one of our favorite instructions in scripture is to "speak the truth in love," a passage that has been used to justify offending many.

The frustrations we have when communicating between sexes can give you a glimpse into the potential conflicts arising when these two forms of communication interact. Men tend to prefer direct communication; women tend to prefer more of an indirect style. "That's not what I said," the direct communicator insists. "But that's what you meant," the indirect communicator retorts.

Ni-Vanuatu value indirect communication. A skilled orator always beats around the bush. Their overriding objective in communication is maintaining unity, not clarity. They may correct someone who has made a mistake, insult someone who has made them angry, or slap down someone who has gotten cocky, but for the most part, they do so in a way that gives plausible deniability. If maintaining unity requires ambiguity, then that is acceptable collateral damage.

In this context, an unenthusiastic yes means no. Vague, indefensible excuses are to be accepted at face value because they cloak a real, legitimate issue. Repeated questions yield not clarification but the answer it is believed the questioner wants to hear. To many Americans, this is not communication at all. At worst it is lying, at best a murky mess of confusion. In truth it is a code, and like all codes, it can yield the truth or a lie. Indirect communication in itself is not deception. You just have to know the code.

An American's problems understanding indirect communication are nothing compared to the blunders we make attempting to communicate with others in this environment. Ni-Vanuatu use direct communication only with those they consider too simpleminded to grasp indirect communication: children, idiots, and dogs.

In our desperate need for clarity, we spell everything out, giving explicit instructions and seeking affirmation that our hearers understand. What we intend as simple instructions, loving correction, needed clarification, constructive criticism, or even a brilliantly clear sermon is understood as insulting and disrespectful by Ni-Vanuatu. Why? We must intend to offend them; why else would we speak to them like dogs?

On the next descent, I followed Norman's "description" of my good driving. Slipping the truck into four-wheel-drive low, I shifted to first and crept down the mountainside, easily avoiding the gaping potholes and navigating my way over the deep ruts. This time the truck remained firmly in my control, gravel didn't spray wildly from the tires, and there was no panic. When we reached the bottom, Chief Norman smiled. "See what I mean, missionary? You are a very good driver."

Medicine is a Long Way from Us

The small thatch hut is divided into multiple exam rooms by brightly colored sarongs. The roof overhead is sharply pitched; it rises a little more than eight feet at the center of the house, falling to meet the outside wall at three feet from the floor. The wall is woven with freshly cut bamboo, still a deep jungle green. The rustic floor is made up of rough wooden planks with wide gaps between them.

A small bamboo bench runs along the low side wall; a folding chair and a precarious table the size of a TV tray occupies the center of the little exam room. A flashlight hangs from a bamboo rafter above, painting a small circle of bright light on the table and yielding a dim glow to the rest of the room.

The patients occupy the bamboo bench; a father, a mother, and a handful of children. They are dressed in the local custom, which means that they are far more undressed than dressed. The father and mother sit on the bench while the kids jostle around them for position. Their dark-brown skin spotted with white rings of fungal infections. The children's round bellies protrude out in front of them, displaying a lack of nutrition or possibly severe infestations of worms. Thick green mucus drains from their noses and lines their upper lips. Deep hacking coughs shake little ribcages. Wide eyes take in the doctor and missionary, strange foreigners who wear clothes.

Dr. Yumi, all of five foot three, was forced to stand hunched over under the sloping roofline. She stands just outside the pale circle of light from the flashlight and listens as I translate the health concerns of the family. The symptoms are vague and sometimes difficult to translate. "My body is sore" could mean just about anything. She begins her exam, all the while asking questions.

Some questions that are obvious to an American are nearly incomprehensible to Ni-Vanuatu. I see the bewilderment in the father's eyes when I translate the doctor's query concerning the color of bowel movements. I am sure it is a very valid diagnostic tool to know such things. But how does a person who uses an outhouse and no toilet paper even begin to know such a thing? The father hesitated before answering that they were the color of feces. Aren't they all the same color? Apparently he coached the later patients concerning the types of questions the doctor would ask; throughout the afternoon, we heard a veritable rainbow of answers to this question.

One issue with short-term clinics like this one is the need for follow-up. The doctor can give the initial treatment, but often the patient will need a follow-up appointment and possibly continued treatment. "Do they have a clinic in the village where they are from?" Dr. Yumi asks. When I translate this question to the father, he shakes his head slowly, explaining that they have walked an hour this morning just so they could see the doctor. "Missionary, medicine is a long way from us," he replies.

Indeed, medicine is a long way from them. There are four hospitals with doctors and dentists present in Vanuatu: four hospitals for more than sixty-five islands. Those fortunate enough to live on one of the four islands with a hospital can expect to see a doctor if they are seriously ill. Those who live on one of the sixty-one islands without a hospital or who live in remote areas of the larger islands depend on a widely spread system of village clinics and health centers, where they seek the services of midwives, nurse practitioners, and village health workers.

How widely spread? When we began work on Hope Clinic in Big Bay, a French doctor working for an NGO complained that it was too near other clinics, that we should find a more remote location. I was stunned. The village where the clinic is located is a four-hour drive from town, one hour of which is off road and is frequently cut off from the rest of the island by flooded rivers. "How far apart do you want the clinics to be?" I asked him. He responded that the health NGOs in Vanuatu had determined that clinics should be spaced no closer than twelve hours' walking distance. Can you imagine having to walk six hours to see a village health worker when you are sick?

Physical distance is not the only reason that medicine is far from them. The government of Vanuatu rightly requires that accurate records of patients seen and treatments provided be kept and reported to the health department each month. The clinics and health centers that fail to do so do not receive any additional medicines. While some of the clinics are well run and faithful in their reporting, the sad truth is that record keeping and consistent reporting is often neglected by the health workers. I have visited many of these small aid posts scattered across the islands to discover that they have only a few out-of-date Tylenol tablets sitting on their shelves.

Dr. Yumi retreats from her examination of the patients; there, on the small table, she writes out her diagnoses and instructions for the pharmacy. She prescribes worming medicine, antifungal cream, and a grocery list of other items to this family. She gives a few words of instruction and caution concerning the medicines and recommends a follow-up, regardless of how far they must walk.

Before handing them their prescriptions, she asks, "Can I pray with you?" As we bow our heads to pray in that simple day clinic, we are reminded that medicine may be a long way from them, but God is not.

Snake Vines

I walk through a thick stand of tropical ebony with my eyes elevated. I focus high up in the canopy. I am looking for the telltale signs of trees with rotten centers. With ebony the most common cause of a rotten heart is a branch that has broken off and rotted, creating a pathway for decay into the tree. Such trees typically have a water stain on their trunk high up in their crown.

I stumble over a thick tangle of roots and vines. Beneath this living mesh, the ground is boggy mud. Not watching where I am going causes numerous stumbles. But my stumbling is not in vain: I find a beautiful specimen. Its trunk, straight and true, stretches thirty feet before the first branch. Five feet wide at its base, it has a very slow taper along its trunk. Its bark, healthy and free from blemishes, gives me confidence it's a healthy tree.

I slowly circle the tree at a distance. It looks good from all sides. I expect to get a lot of timber here. Timber, especially termite-proof timber, is vital. I am in the early stages of the construction of Hope Clinic, a medical clinic and nurses' house deep in the bush of Big Bay, Santo. The clinic site is essentially a small rise in the middle of a swamp. In the raining season, it will be the only dry spot for miles: termite heaven. Hauling treated lumber from town is not practical. So, equipped with a portable sawmill, I am preparing to cut solid tropical hardwoods that are impervious to bugs.

Chief Robert and his sons, Paul and Norman, accompany me. They are the ones who have taught me to distinguish between the various species. Experienced in cutting timber themselves, they taught me the signs to avoid. Satisfied with the tree before me, yet still unsure of my own ability to evaluate standing timber, I call to them for their endorsement. Paul and Norman readily concur with my choice. "Hemi nao!" they exclaim. "That's the one!"

Chief Robert slowly approaches, displeased that I am even considering cutting the ebony. His choice is a large rosewood several kilometers away. While I appreciate the beauty of rosewood, accessing it would be complex. It would require cutting a road through the jungle and swamp. Then the mill and resulting timber would have to be hauled through the resulting mire. This stand of ebony, on the other hand, sits just below the building site.

Chief Robert takes one look at my choice and immediately voices his disapproval. "No, missionary, won't work. This one has a rotten center," he curtly proclaims. I look the tree over again, trying to see what I missed in my earlier inspection. Nothing. I glance back to Paul and Robert. They have thinly veiled looks of disgust on their faces.

The chief moves on to inspect other trees, and I query Norman with my eyes. "There's nothing wrong with the tree," he answers. "See that large vine hanging from the branches? It's called a snake vine. He believes it hosts a dangerous spirit, that if, as we cut the tree, the vine breaks, the spirit will be released, and someone in the village will die."

Suddenly I understand Chief Robert's reticence for me to cut in this grove. Nearly every tree features the thick, heavy looping creepers of the snake vine. To him I am not merely cutting timber. I am invading a stronghold of local spirits and inviting disaster into the community. Even if I find a vine-free tree, its fall will surely break the vine of a neighboring tree. I groan, head back to my truck, and prepare to cut a road to the rosewood.

Thirteen years later, I am with another chief in Big Bay, though he doesn't use the title "chief." He goes by Elder Noah. He considers his position in the church far more significant than the trappings of being a chief. He and I are sitting in the cold water of a rushing mountain stream beside his village of Pemau. Around us, dozens of kids are playing in a natural water park.

I watch toddlers and their mothers splashing in the shallow fan at the bottom of the pool downstream. The children splash enthusiastically while their mothers search the rocks for shellfish and freshwater prawns. Beside me preteen boys perfect their diving technique by racing down a sandy beach, leaping over a stick hurdle, and plunging into the rushing water. Upstream, teenagers and young adults climb high up a broken rock face, grasp thick vines, and swing out over the deep end of the pool before engaging in duels high above the water or twisting into spectacular dives. The trees the vines are tied to bob and weave under their weight.

I can't help but be impressed with the stoutness of the vines. The ends have been split and tied around the branches of trees that sprout from the rock face and hang far out over the stream. I keep waiting for one of them to come untied or to snap in mid-swing, but in spite of being used hundreds of times, they seem as strong at the end of the day as at the beginning.

I turn to Elder Noah. "Wanem kaen rop ia? What kind of vine is that?" I ask.

Nonchalantly he answers, "Snake vine."

He goes on to explain. "Every morning I go and cut fresh ones so that the kids can swing on them. They are the strongest vines and work best for swinging." My mind goes back to Chief Robert's fear. What an amazing contrast: one chief insists on us adding a week's worth of work to avoid snake vines, another cuts them every day for the village children to play on.

Vanuatu hosts over one hundred different languages, and each tribe has a slightly different culture and spiritual beliefs. I know that Noah and Robert speak different languages, so I wonder if their tribes have different views regarding these vines. I tell Noah the story of Robert's fears, without mentioning names, and ask if his tribe has similar views. "Yes, missionary," he answers, "but we have Jesus. We don't have to be afraid of the spirits anymore."

Vinmavis

The road disappears into the ocean. To my left sits an imposing cliff, its craggy face covered with a dense tangle of foliage broken only by rough barren projections of stone. To my right a calm body of water lays sheltered in the gently curving arms of a bay. The rock face on my left angles toward the beach and, before me, edges its pointed face into the water. Ahead of me and gently sloping to the right, two softly rutted tracks make their way across a white sand beach before slipping into the ocean. I stop the truck in confusion. Surely this isn't the end of the road.

We are headed to the village of Vinmavis on the island of Malakula—a beachside village that sits half a mile from the sea, home to amazingly abundant lobster, a passionate church, the largest thatch school building I have ever seen, and warm, friendly people. I have been told this road leads to Vinmavis and assured that one could drive all the way to the village. Inwardly I groan, sure that this was to be yet another example of how, far too often, reality in Vanuatu doesn't quite reflect what you are told. Ni-Vanuatu tend to soften the blows so that you don't get discouraged ahead of time!

I prepare to park the truck, anticipating a hike over the cliff face in order to reach the village. Falau, my friend and guide for the day, stops me. "No, no, misinari, rod ia nao. Don't stop, missionary; this is the road," he says, pointing ahead into the bay. I am stunned. The road is through the ocean? I slip the truck into four-wheel-drive low, whisper a prayer for forgiveness for the damage I am about to do to my truck, and drive out into the gentle waves.

I round the towering point of stone, with the sand and coral softly crunching beneath my tires and waves lapping at my sideboards. On the other side of the point, the cliff is split in two; a huge cube-shaped boulder lays with one corner deeply buried in the sand and a second corner nearly touching the cliff face that had birthed it. Between this massive stone and the cliff, a narrow strip of white sand is marked with tire tracks. As the truck climbs the beach and slips through the narrow opening between the two stone walls, I feel like I am entering a secret garden. A short time later, we rounded the last curve and pulled into the village of Vinmavis.

Vinmavis is laid out in neat rows; each hut, accompanied by a small separate kitchen, sits in a yard enclosed by a trim hedge. Between the rows of huts are wide pathways of white sand carefully cleared of grass and leaves. Each yard is adorned with flowering plants: brilliant red, yellow, and purple hibiscus or deep peach and crimson bougainvilleas. It is a clean, tidy village filled with warm, smiling people. Women crouch beside open fires in their kitchens, chatting with their sisters, cousins, or friends. Peals of laughter punctuate their conversations. Children race hand in hand down the sandy pathways, bouncing cheerful giggles off the huts they pass. Men gather in the shade of massive mango or *nambangga* trees, their conversation a quiet murmur broken by sedate, understated chuckles.

Pastor Tonsi leads us to our home in Vinmavis, a two-room thatch hut. This hut features a cement floor. Its walls of woven bamboo are interrupted with casement-style windows whose panes are also bamboo. A small stick serves to prop these windows open, allowing a welcome breeze in the tropical night. Nets hanging over thin foam mattresses provide a nighttime escape from hungry mosquitoes.

A hundred yards from our hut, a ring of trees forms a curtain between us and the ocean. It is comprised of the typical seaside mix of coconut palms, pandanas, and ironwood. Eager to see the ocean view near our new home, I weave my way through the tangle of branches into the open expanse of white sand. Before me the beach slopes sharply down and ends in...stone. A flat, barren, broken and scarred expanse of stone stretches out a half a mile before abruptly dropping off into the ocean.

Many years before, Vinmavis sat on the seashore. The waves lapped gently at this beach where I now stand. A massive earthquake struck early one morning. The ocean pulled violently away from the beach. The villagers, recognizing the signs of an impending tsunami, fled for the hills overlooking the village. There they waited fearfully.

They expected at any moment to see a wall of water surge over the newly exposed reef, up the gentle slope of their beach, and through their village. They expected to see houses broken up by the waves, roofs floating free, cherished possessions bobbing in a thick mat of flotsam, pigs, and chickens scrambling for their lives. They waited to see the church filled with rushing seawater, to see the school flooded and textbooks and desks washed away. They waited, but the wall of water never came.

That day Malakula tipped on its axis. Vinmavis was lifted, its extensive coral reef thrust into the air, where its vibrantly colored corals soon died and faded to a dull gray. To the east, small islands that sat on the same underlying shelf as Malakula found themselves suddenly plunged beneath the sea. Entire islands, complete with villages, churches, and gardens, dropped suddenly beneath the waves. Mothers scrambled in the deluge to save their children; fathers floundered in the chaos looking for their families; villages were overcome in a matter of seconds, their residents unable to grasp the impending doom signaled by the violent shaking of the ground. For those villages, it was a powerful earthquake, a flood of seawater, frothy, churning waves followed by an awful silence broken only by the wails of the few survivors clinging to debris.

Today Vinmavis is a vibrant village. To the east, across the mountainous spine of Malakula, a restless ocean hides a lost island. The posts of its houses still stand beneath the waves as lonely sentinels. There, no cooking fires burn, no women gossip, no children race, no fathers return from their gardens, and no stone marks the place of their watery burial. As I stand on Vinmavis's sandy shore watching the sun sink into the waves in the west, the dull-gray slab of rock stretching out before me is the only memorial to a vanquished isle.

McKenzie's Candle

Tabuna stared through the inky darkness. He and his brothers, uncles, and cousins crouched low among the *biglif* vines, waiting in anticipation. Tabuna held a thick, heavy *nalnal*, a deadly club. Others carried an assortment of nalnals, spears, and knives. Tonight when the missionary slept, he would die.

Arriving in Vanuatu in 1895, James Noble McKenzie choose Hokua as his second base of operations. From the hilltop towering over the community and Cape Cumberland, he could see the steep approach on all sides and far out to sea, east into Big Bay, north and west far out over the rolling ocean. It was a gorgeous location. Fresh sea breezes provided relief from the damp tropical heat. The small rise provided enough altitude and drainage to offer protection from malaria.

Here he dug out a simple basement, lined it with stones, and built a home for his family. Patiently he cleared the yard and constructed a stone fence. A passing steamer had unloaded a 250-gallon iron tank to the small harbor below the village. Earlier today he had convinced the local chief to fill the tank with water and carry it to his small house on the hill.

A huge crowd gathered to view this massive contraption. Once the tank was filled with fresh water, McKenzie climbed on top. The chief organized the men; poles were gathered, vines tied into a thick supporting network, and then with shouts, grunts, and cheers, the men lifted the tank and began the trek up the steep hillside. I'm sure that for McKenzie it was a great day; finally he would have a secure supply of water. Unbeknown to him, the chief and the men plotted his death as they climbed.

What kept them from killing him on the trail? What chance would one man have of defending himself against so many? Why did they go to the work of carrying him and a thousand liters of water up the hillside while planning his murder? Was it a fear of the unknown?

Melanesians have a distinct view of causation. They see a physical world underpinned by a vast network of spiritual links on "the other side of the leaf." Events that disturb this network are believed to affect reality in seemingly unrelated areas. For example, anger due to an unresolved dispute between two parties is believed to contaminate the physical environment in such a way as to cause illness in innocent third parties.

Thus, they are extremely cautious when encountering the unknown. They knew and understood the hazards of attacking a local spiritual leader, or *kleva*, and had developed strategies mitigating the danger. The missionary represented an unknown. He clearly had spiritual powers. What unforeseen events might happen if he had the opportunity to use them in his defense?

As the men carried their burden up the hill, the chief approved a plan to kill the missionary while he slept. However, he insisted that they wait till the missionary's cooking fire had died to ensure that he and his family were truly asleep. Tabuna and his fellow porters gave lusty shouts of excitement. Tomorrow they would feast on the missionary and his family.

Crouching low in the vines and brush just outside the mission yard, Tabuna and his coconspirators watched the flickering light in the window of the mission house. Coarse whispers described their intentions; boasts were made, plans developed and then rehashed. Overhead the stars wheeled in a cloudless sky; half the night passed, but still the light flickered.

Muscles overworked in the day stiffened in the cool night air. Sleep began to overcome the adrenaline rush of the planned ambush. Still the missionary refused to sleep. Sensing he was losing his men's enthusiasm, the chief called off the attack.

What had gone wrong? Had the missionary somehow divined their intentions? Had his past experiences at the mission station Nogugu taught him extreme caution? "Tomorrow," the chief assured his men, "tomorrow he will be too tired to maintain a watch. We kill him then."

Night after night, Tabuna and his cousins crouched in the bush. Night after night, they rehearsed the attack in muted mutters. Night after night, as they prepared for bed, Mrs. McKenzie lit a long tapered candle in the candle holder on the rude wooden table. As the McKenzies slept, it flickered in the tropical breezes, casting its dim light through the window, convincing the would-be murderers someone was still awake, patiently pushing sticks in the fire.

Mawe, one of the great-great-grandchildren of the frustrated conspirators, tells me how after weeks of thwarted attacks, the village abandoned the idea of killing the missionary and instead accepted him and the message he brought.

He takes me up the hill to McKenzie's homestead. Today thick brush covers the former mission yard. The stone fence is a barely discernible bump in the thick carpet of vines that covers any gaps in the trees. A few deft strokes of a bush knife reveal the patiently arranged stones. The house has rotted away; the carefully dug basement with its dry stacked-stone walls and a bit of the rusty metal from the water tank are all that remain.

Mawe tells me, "The fact that my ancestors had never seen a candle before saved the missionaries' lives." He insists that on dark moonless nights, you can still see McKenzie's candle flickering there among the trees.

I stand there in the jungle of what used to be a mission station. I am sure I can feel the tension of the first few nights. As I handle the rusty bits of the water tank, I can envision that fateful day. When I step into the simple basement, I can see roughhewn shelves full of foodstuffs. The atmosphere of the place is alive with history. It's no wonder it has a mystical pull on Mawe and his fellow villagers.

Does McKenzie's candle still burn? No, I don't believe any paranormal apparition appears here on moonless nights. But in a real way, McKenzie's candle does still burn. It burns up and down the west coast of Santo when thousands of villagers gather each Sunday to worship.

Home

I hate an empty house.

I step into the house to make one final inspection. My footsteps echo in rooms without furniture, bounce off of walls without decorations and windows without curtains. The house sits empty and still. Yet I am sure I can feel the reverb of the sounds that once vibrated through this house. I stand perfectly still and quiet and feel with all my might. I'm sure I can feel the rapidly fading effects of my family's time here.

I want to make sure there is nothing left behind. I methodically open each kitchen cabinet and drawer. I squat to inspect the bathroom vanity. I peer on tiptoes at top shelves in closets. As I make my examination, I do my best to ignore a gnawing sensation in the center of my chest.

The house is clear; nothing of value has been left. But something priceless yet very intangible has been. I stand in the living room, sure that I can hear the screams of laughter of my playing children. I walk into the kitchen and taste on the air the rich aromas of Renee's cooking. In the bathroom, I catch the scent of feminine bath products. I step into our bedroom; a faint whiff of perfume lingers there, flooding my mind with memories. In my sons' bedroom, I lean against a crayon-decorated wall, close my eyes, and see a floor strewn with toys and towheaded boys sprawled in sleep.

As I walk through the house for the last time, I let my fingers linger and slip over the smooth walls, finding that my fingertips are almost but not quite sensitive enough to divine the echo of conversations from the time that we have shared here. Something is here, intangible, elusive, lingering just outside my grasp. A segment of my life, shared with my wife and children, remains.

This has been our home. It is full of memories and scents. Its very air seems saturated with the waves of emotion that have been felt here, as if somehow they spilled out of us and altered our physical environment. A place of prayer still has a sacred feel. The kitchen still carries the joy of meals shared and the stress of problems tackled here. The worry wrestled with at the side of a child's sickbed seems to linger in the room.

I stand in the middle of the living room and close my eyes. I breathe in deeply, willing the flood of memories, the aftershock of emotions and lingering scents into myself. I valiantly try to capture the essence of this home, to bottle it within me—because when I walk out that door, it will be gone. I am leaving. This is not my home.

I hate an empty house.

As a child, I grew up in the same home my mother had lived in prior to marrying my father. Every part of the house, every bit of the yard was pregnant with memories. My grandfather had planted that tree, my granny had planted those roses. My aunts had grown up in those bedrooms. My parents had courted in that living room. Christmases were shared, birthdays celebrated, wedding announcements made in that house. It was there I met my future in-laws, that I asked my wife to marry me and watched my parents share the heartrending grief of losing a child. I remember watching my father's face crumple with pain as he looked out the window of the front door and realized that my brother would never come bounding up those steps again.

As a child, I never experienced the uprooting that takes place when a family moves. For me, my home and my house were one and the same. As an adult, I longed to recreate my childhood experience for my children. But this has not been the case. As a missionary, my children have lived in many different homes in three different countries.

I try to minimize the upheaval. In Vanuatu, I built a missions house to save money but also to create some permanence so that each time we returned to the field, we would return to the same home. In the United States, Renee and I purchased a house and have continued to live in it each time we return, moving renters out, restoring the damage they have done, and attempting to recreate the sense of home once again.

It doesn't really work. While we are in Vanuatu, we catch ourselves talking about America as home. When we are Stateside, we find ourselves referring to Vanuatu as home. One of the most complicated questions I get asked is, "Where are you from?" Where am I from? Where is my home?

One day I will step into my new home, and I will never again walk through an empty house.

The Missionary Family

As the truck rolls to a stop, engine noises are replaced with the soft crunch of coral under the tires. Before me, in two narrow white lines, lies the road to Matandas, with its endless black beach. To the right is a coconut plantation where sturdy young palms hold thick clusters of green coconuts. On my left is the Vatthe Conservation Area, a United Nations World Heritage Site and one of the few uncut coastal tropical rainforests in Vanuatu.

A vague track heads off between towering trees on the left. I know where it leads, through dark, musty, deep mud under the perpetual shadow of a continuously dripping canopy. It travels a path closely defined by thick undergrowth of glossy leaves and gnarled, twisted vines that is endlessly refined by fallen rosewoods, ebonies, and teaks.

It breaks free of the forest and emerges onto a gray pebble beach that seems to stretch to the horizons; it follows the beach until it becomes a narrow spit of land with a swamp on one side and the gently rolling ocean on the other. At the mouth of a small river, it abandons the beach to enter a thick grove of *burao*, a low, dense, rough-barked group of trees whose branches bend and twist like contortionists, weaving such a maze that it is impossible to know where one tree ends and another begins.

The track emerges from the burao thicket to weave its way through a stand of wild sugarcane, forming a narrow tunnel through the sharp-edged pale-green leaves of the cane, whose wispy flowers dance in the breeze over twenty feet above. It slides out of its leafy tunnel to glide through cool, clear streams under the shade of mature ironwoods. It bumps over a boulder-strewn floodplain before coming to rest in a grove of juvenile ironwoods.

There, the sound of the Jordan River fills the air like an acoustic fog, obscuring all other sounds. The ground is composed of round gray river stones, packed together like a cobblestone road. Spare strands of dry grasses cling to the sand-filled cracks between the stones, vainly trying to establish a foothold. Young ironwood trees screen the river from view, their long dusky-green needles stirring restlessly in the breeze.

This path covers about four miles as the crow flies and requires a full hour to drive. It is best covered in a four-wheel-drive truck with high clearance, a strong winch, and a steady hand. An adventure for some, a nightmare for others, it is the road to Hope Clinic.

Hope Clinic provides primary medical care for the people of Big Bay. Its purpose is, by compassion, to overcome resistance to the gospel among the villages of the Tiali tribe. Steven and Kara Jeager are serving there, sewing up cuts, treating malaria, and delivering babies. Today is Kara's twenty-first birthday.

Our truck comes to rest at the entrance of the road, and we contemplate it. The truck is filled to overflowing. Our family of six has been joined by two fellow missionaries, giving us eight bodies in a truck designed for five at the most. Gift bags sprouting decorative tissue paper, enough groceries to feed our crew for a day, and a birthday cake in muffin form also crowd the truck. We are on our way to a surprise birthday party—we think.

Two things have foiled our plans: a faulty truck and a transparent husband. A week before, the four-wheel drive on the truck stopped working. I was concerned about trying to slog my way through the mud and then ford the river without it, so I decided to let Steve in on the secret so that he could meet us here before the road gets bad.

It seems, however, that Kara knows Steve a little too well. Even though I gave him an excuse for the phone call, I think our secret lasted less than fifteen minutes after we got off the phone. When he arrives, he lets us know that the element of surprise has been lost, and we pile in the clinic truck for the journey to the river.

We cross the river, some on horseback and some on foot. The ford is just upstream of churning rapids. The Jordan at the ford is cool, clear, smooth, and waist-deep. At the edge, the stones are slippery, covered by moss. As you step into the current, the moss dissipates, giving you more secure footing, but this advantage is canceled out by the intensity of the tide. There is a strategy for crossing safely: plant your walking stick securely, move one foot, verify that you have good footing, move the other foot, ensure that you have good footing there as well, and repeat. Get in a hurry, and you will find yourself tripped up and then submerged.

On the far side of the river, we make our way up a mud bank, through a coconut plantation, and over a muddy hill before entering the village. The village spreads out before us in a huge circle around a five-acre village green. On the far side of the village, inside a tidy fence and a neatly mowed yard, is the church, Hope Clinic, and the missions house, where Steve and Kara make their home.

Inside that little missions house, candles are lit, songs are sung, laughter and gifts are shared. The trip is made, the role of family is played out by surrogates ten thousand miles from home and those we hold dear, because here, as missionaries in a land far from home, we are family.

Fighting Fire with Fire

As we enter the ash plain surrounding Mount Yasur, the landscape is dominated by the huge ash cone of the volcano. Gray with wind-sculptured sides reaching nearly two thousand feet into the sky, it shakes with nearly continuous eruptions. The air is filled with the stench of sulfur, and the raindrops hitting the windshield of the truck are gritty with ash. The ground around us is dotted with chunks of pumice and other lava rocks testifying to the fact that we are well within range of the eruptions.

Once, a vast lake filled the ash plain, wild ducks flocked there, and villagers fished in its waters for a variety of fish, eels, and giant prawns. Then an earthquake in the midst of a rainstorm fractured the ash and lava dam that held back the waters. The accumulated water rushed through the rupture quickly, carved a deep canyon across the floor of the plain, and inundated the village of Sulfur Bay with a deluge of water and ash. With each storm, the river digs deeper into the soft ash, revealing the fascinating history of eruptions in its canyon walls.

Today the river is raging. The torrential rains we have experienced all day have engorged it, causing it to dig rapidly into its soft bed. We make our way down the side of the canyon to see if it will be possible to cross over. The water is opaque with ash, the surface turbulent, rolling with fury. Occasional chunks of lava weighing hundreds of pounds bounce in the tide, thrown by the water as if they were a child's toy. There is no crossing tonight.

Regretfully, we turn back to the village of Gilgal to spend the night with Pastor Obed and his wife. Maybe tomorrow the river will be crossable. The rain continues to pummel us when we reach the village, and everyone makes a mad dash from the truck to the church. Clothing is soaked, backpacks are drenched; it is going to be a cold, damp night. We are thankful for the shelter of the church.

The church at Gilgal is a very simple structure. The floor is fine volcanic ash, the walls are made of badly rusted corrugated iron, and the roof is made of grass. The only light comes from the windows and door—or really, the open spaces where they should be. There are no chairs or benches of any kind. The platform is a line of cinder blocks arranged in a rough square at the front of the church, with more ash shoveled into the middle to create a surface six inches higher than the rest of the church. The pulpit is a single board mounted on two bamboo legs buried in the ash.

There is the initial flurry of unpacking as we spread out wet clothes over every available surface, hoping against hope that they will somehow dry. Soon we are reduced to boredom—staring out at the driving rain, wondering how long it will delay our building the new church at Iatapu. I turn my attention to the church building. The roof of the church appears new, but the posts that support it are aged and scarred by fire. I am curious; I know that a few months earlier, Pastor Obed's home was burned. Was the church burned as well?

Wet clothes and a strong breeze chill everyone, and we make our way to the pastor's kitchen. There we cluster around the small fire in the center of the floor, munch on *namambe*, a large, nearly tasteless nut, tell stories, and laugh at jokes. I watch as Pastor Obed's wife and daughters scramble to prepare food for thirteen unexpected guests. I step out into the rain to ask the pastor's wife if they will have enough food, and offer to pay for some if there is any in the village to be purchased. "Don't worry," she tells me. "Pastor Obed is on his way with corn."

Soon Pastor Obed strides into the churchyard. He is a short wiry man, all bone, sinew, and muscle. His face is lined with deep creases, his mouth filled with far too few teeth. Equipped with a booming voice, a passion for souls, and unflappable optimism, he is nicknamed "Obed Natora" by his fellow pastors— "Old Ironsides," if we were to put it into English. He steps into the small kitchen, his hair and clothes soaked with rain, a bundle of corn over his shoulder, bouncing "Praise the Lord" and "Halleluiah" off the walls.

Eager hands reach out for the corn, and it is thrown, husk and all, onto the coals of the fire. Smoke fills the kitchen, and I escape to the church, looking for fresh air.

Shortly after my escape, Pastor Obed comes to the church with two freshly roasted ears of corn. We begin gnawing on the tough kernels. I ask him about the burn marks on the posts of the church. "Pastor," I begin, "I thought the last time I visited you, your house had just been burned. Did I misunderstand? Was it the church that burned instead?"

"No, no, they burned my church and then my house, Praise the Lord!" he nearly shouts. "That was the second time they have burned the church, but buildings, they really don't matter. Missionary, let me tell you the vision that God showed me when they burned us out," and he begins to tell me of an outpouring of the Holy Spirit God has promised him.

As I listen to his story, I have to smile. Here is a pastor who is determined to fight fire with Fire.

Big Man

My plastic chair is positioned under the shade of a leaning mango tree. The narrow legs of the chair rapidly sink into the sand, forcing me to adjust and reorient the chair every few minutes. Before me a small table is loaded with the best of the food the village has to offer: fresh pineapple, bananas, hot tapioca *lap lap* smothered in coconut cream, freshly grilled melt-in-your-mouth steaks, a huge pork roast—far more food than I can eat.

The table and my chair are situated on a narrow strip of sand in the lee of a massive stone that juts out into a river. Before me lies a shimmering pool of cold, crystal-clear water. The sand slips slowly below the surface, creating a gently sloping floor for the pool till it faces the unabated current just beyond the reach of the stone. There the sand disappears into turquoise waters.

Above and below the pool, the river snags on clusters of stones, yielding frothing white water, miniature waterfalls, and singing rapids. The roar of the water drowns out everything but the mirthful shrieks of children at play. The far bank of the river is strewn with massive boulders, interspersed with gnarled trees on a canvas of steeply sloping moss-covered rock face. Thick vines hang from the uppermost branches of the trees.

Dozens of screaming, laughing children play in the pool. They leap from the stones near me. Some play tag while others bend low over the surface, searching for shellfish. Others scramble up the broken rock face, clutch the thick vines, and swing high over the clear shimmering pool before engaging in impossible flips and dives. One enterprising little boy splashes through the rapids at the tail of the pool on a pair of homemade stilts. Another chattering group climbs high in the trees over the pool and dangles like a troop of monkeys from the thick looping vines in the crown of the trees.

As a father of four, I know that when children play this hard, they develop ravenous appetites. Yet none of the children approach the table. Not one of them so much as glance at the steaming food. They don't dare. Protocol is deeply engrained in children of Vanuatu. Regardless of how I feel as a father, I am an honored guest. At mealtimes, I am unapproachable. Yet there is more than enough food; clearly, I can't eat it all.

Noah is a big man. Taller, broader, and heavier than anyone else in the village, Noah is a "Big Man." He is the chief and the sole landowner. Everyone else in the village lives on and farms his land. He is the final court of appeals for local disputes. His wide face breaks into a broad gap-toothed grin as he approaches me. His large body lurches back and forth as he negotiates the steep hillside dropping to the narrow beach. Slightly out of breath, he grunts and points to the heavily laden table. "Pretty good, huh? You like it?" I lavish praise on the spread, the cooks, and the scenery.

He removes the leaf covering the pork roast and pushes stubby fingers deep into the meat. He pries a thick wedge loose from the pork and looks at me almost sheepishly. "You don't mind if I have some, do you? Kinda hungry." I urge him to take all he wants. After all, it came from his gardens and farm. I am a bit taken aback by the amount of pork he has pulled off the roast. "How can one man eat so much?" I wonder. "No wonder he's fat," I think to myself.

In Vanuatu few people are overweight, much less obese. If you see someone who is overweight, it is a clear sign of power. Everyone else works hard for their food. Walk through town, and if you spot an obese man, odds are you are looking at a member of parliament or a staff member of a cabinet minister. When campaign season heats up, the coffee shops are perpetually filled with thick, heavy men purchasing beer and ice cream for potential voters.

It's all about resources. Those without power have little or no access to them. Those inside the circles of power and influence drive large trucks, eat lavish meals in restaurants, travel abroad, send their kids to the best schools, keep a mistress or two: Big Men.

At least that's the simplistic view of Big Men most Westerners hold. The lucky few consume a disproportionate amount of resources while their fellow countrymen struggle along in poverty. The truth is more complex than that. Big Men do have access to resources that others can only dream about, and sometimes they consume more than they should, but that is not the Ni-Vanuatu concept of a Big Man. To Ni-Vanuatu a Big Man is a leader.

In the book *Yumi* Reuben Makikon, the first chairman of the Vanuatu Christian Council and a recognized leader in Vanuatu, describes this leadership as becoming "aware of the needs of others" and "to take initiative to be responsible for others." He insists that anyone can become a leader, "as soon as you become sensitive to the needs of your people."

Noah stepped away from the table, holding the thick, greasy clump of pork in his hands. He broke off a small piece, chewed on it thoughtfully, and slowly waded out into the pool full of children. They clustered around him like minnows, eagerly accepting pieces of the rich meat that moments before had been inaccessible to them. The powerful used his privilege to access resources beyond the grasp of the powerless so that all could share in the richness of the table. A Big Man, Vanuatu style.

Before You Ask

The sky is gray and heavy. A cool breeze blows across the channel, filling the air with the scent of salt. The sun is rising, but only a dull-gray light filters through, painting the world in black and white with just a hint of color. After three days of constant rain, I am not optimistic about today. Today is the day we are to pour the floor for Nathan and Jennifer Thomas's house.

I check my to-do list lying on the passenger seat before heading out. I have too many tools and need too many workers to take them all in one trip, thus the predawn trip. Worries rattle around in my mind, competing for attention. Will it rain? Will I have enough workers? Will the materials that have been promised actually be delivered? Will the ground at the building site be too soggy for the truck to drive over? Will the cement mixer break down before the pour is finished?

I often ask myself how it is that I have become a builder. My mind goes back to the initial interview that I had during my application to become a missionary. In a skill assessment, I had given myself a zero on mechanical and building skills. Cary Tidwell, then the head of personnel, had questioned me on this. "You do know that missionaries often have to be a jack-of-all-trades?" he asked.

I remember holding up both hands with my fingers spread. "They may look like fingers," I told him, "but really they are all thumbs." Yet today,

I somehow find myself currently engaged in seven major building projects and building the third house of my missionary career.

Today my biggest concern is workers. Building with all volunteers creates its own set of challenges. You never know how many workers you may have on a given day. You train one set of workers to use particular tools to accomplish a certain task and then find that the next time you are engaged in that task, you have an entirely different set of workers that you must train all over again. Motivating volunteers is complex. You can't push them; you must lead by example and try to challenge them to outwork you.

Today my primary concern is just having enough workers. Mixing and pouring cement is heavy work needing plenty of hands, and the threat of rain is enough to make most volunteers decide to stay close to the fire. "Please, God," I pray, "just once could I have sufficient money to hire enough workers?"

At the campus toolshed, I hurriedly unload the tools we will need for the day while keeping a weather eye on the sky. Thus far, the clouds merely threaten rain. As I walk to the work site, about three hundred yards away, my feet sink down into the thick, gooey mud spawned by the weekend's downpours. "Lord, how are they going to get the sand and gravel in here? Do I need to wait for another day?" I finish my prayer by asking for plenty of sunshine to dry out the mud, and then hurry back to town to pick up as many workers as I can before the building materials are scheduled to arrive.

In town my fears are confirmed. People are worried about rain. I go to the first two of three designated pickup spots for volunteers; I come away with a total of four workers—not encouraging. "Missionary, are we going to Nambualu?" they ask. Nambualu, the third pickup spot, is the church where I am currently serving as the interim pastor. We normally pick up two or three workers there. "No," I answer, "the chief said he was bringing their workers today." I am thankful for the help since it saves me a half hour of driving.

I arrive to find that the sand has already been delivered and dumped by the toolshed, not the building site. We load the truck with sand. I begin what I calculate will be over twenty trips hauling sand and gravel for the day. As we pull into Nathan and Jennifer's yard, I feel the mud pulling on the tires; the truck slips to the side, and the wheels begin to spin. The four-wheel drive went out on the truck last week, and without it, I am soon stuck. It is starting to look like a long day. I cross my arms over the steering wheel and bow my head to pray. "Lord, I can't do this. Not with just the five of us and a worn-out truck. Help, Lord!"

My prayer is interrupted by a horn honking and shouts. Coming into the driveway of the campus is the chief's truck—not with the normal two or three workers but with twenty. A laughing, rowdy group of young men converge on my truck, pushing it free of the mud. Bush knives flash in the early morning light, and a new road is cut through the brush, connecting the toolshed and the work site. Shovels fly, loading sand and gravel into the chief's truck. The cement mixer roars to life; ready hands load sand, gravel, cement, and water. Wheelbarrows heavy with cement dig deep ruts in the muddy ground.

The clouds remain, but the rain never comes, and four hours later, I stand back in amazement to see the work is done. I think back to my interrupted prayer this morning and the words of Christ: "For your Father knoweth what things ye have need of, before ye ask him."

Warm and Well Fed

I ease myself down onto the worn and heavily marked fiberboard floor and take the time to look around the small room. It consists of a low ceiling adorned with an empty light socket, three solid walls decorated with an astonishing amount of penciled graffiti, and one wall of rusty metal grating. Two sets of bunk beds press hard against the grating in a futile attempt to capture any breeze. A blanket draped in one corner hides a bucket latrine. Welcome to the high-risk section of Luganville Correctional Center.

Hot, humid air hangs heavy and still. Though one wall is open, there is no other exit, so not even a hint of wind moves through the room. Each choking breath is rancid with the smells of body odor, unwashed linens, and the contents of the bucket. Three inmates glance at me with casual interest from their bunks. The fourth, my former employee, focuses everywhere but on me. This is not where he had planned on seeing me next, certainly not where he intended to spend the next several years of his life. The tension is as thick as the air. Where does one even begin this conversation?

Important conversations in Bislama are almost always conducted at only a few decibels above a whisper. I decide this occasion calls for a subdued but cheerful tone of voice. Acting as if we were meeting beneath a shade tree on one of Luganville's streets, I take the initiative and begin talking about my life during the two-year interval since we have last seen each other. Slowly his eyes find mine. A faint smile crosses his face as I describe each of the kids and how they have grown.

Throwing aside all pretense, he relates the tale of his crime and incarceration. There is not even a trace of bluff, no false protests of innocence. We know each other far too well for such feigning. He brutally raped a young woman; now he will pay the price. I am surprised to find myself torn; as a husband, as a father of a precious daughter, as a man who believes one key measure of a man's character is how he relates to women, I have no sympathy for rapists. Yet this man sitting beside me is more than a former employee. He is my friend.

Metal clangs harshly as the guard rattles the door and gruffly announces, "Time's up!" My friend reaches for my hand. "Will you come back?" he asks. The Holy Spirit whispers the answer in my soul. "I was sick and in prison, and you visited me." I find myself smiling and offering to return weekly for a time of Bible study and prayer. The door rattles impatiently again as I stand. "Next week," I promise.

The first week, my friend and his three cellmates cluster around me on the dirty floor, and together we begin to explore the book of Ephesians. The following week, I discover that the walls are not really solid. A bit of walling is subtly moved to reveal a fist-sized passage to a neighboring cell, first one, then another and yet another. Three ears press against the passages, eager to join the study of God's word.

Following the first week's study, I asked the men to ponder any questions or prayer requests that they might have so that we can engage in a bit of question and answer before a time of prayer. As time begins to run low, I ask about the prayer requests. My friend looks around the room, gathers the unspoken assent of his cellmates, and ventures, "We discussed that, missionary. You know, normally we prisoners spend our time praying that our sentence will be reduced. But what we would really like you to pray about is our families. You see, while we are locked away, we can't provide the food, clothing, and school fees that they need. Would you pray that God will meet their needs?"

I feel like I have been kicked in the gut. My friend grew up without a father. He has six kids. Years before, after a particularly hazardous day's work, he shared with me that his greatest fear was that someday his kids would have to grow up like himself, without a dad. His fear has been realized. True, it is his fault. But what did his kids do to deserve this?

I thought of his boys, the last time I had seen them: a tangled knot of knees and elbows giggling and jostling across their front yard in pursuit of a well-worn and stained soccer ball. My mind flashed to an image of his youngest, just a baby, snuggled against her mother's breast. I wondered how their mother was putting food on the table and what their clothes looked like now. With their father incarcerated, how could their mother possibly raise enough money to pay for six sets of school fees?

"Would you pray that God will meet their needs?" His question burned a hole in my soul. I know that prayer is powerful. But I felt like a hypocrite, mouthing the words. As I prayed, pitiful faces and children dressed in tattered clothing paraded through my mind. I could barely stammer my way through a prayer.

As I stumbled out of the dark cell into the bright tropical sunshine, I felt the words of James 2:15–16 being pressed into my soul like a searing brand: "If a brother or sister is poorly clothed and lacking in daily food, and one of you says to them, 'Go in peace, **be warmed and filled,**' without giving them the things needed for the body, **what good is that?**" And James 1:27: "Pure religion and undefiled before God and the Father is this, To visit the fatherless and widows in their affliction, and to keep himself unspotted from the world."

As a missionary, I don't have funds budgeted for clothing, food, and school fees for the children of prisoners. There is no way I can personally meet the needs of every child of each of these men. I don't know what I am going to do to meet this need. But I know I must do something.

The New Samnalikan

In Vanuatu there are three islands where custom tribes live: Santo, Pentecost, and Tanna. *Custom* is the word used to describe those who follow traditional beliefs. Sometimes we refer to them as pre-Christian. They are not Christian today, but we believe that God desires for them to be.

On each of these three islands, the custom people have preserved the traditional means of dress. On the island of Santo, the custom men wear a *malmal*, basically a loincloth. I'm not sure why, but they seem to prefer bright floral patterns for these clothes. One of my favorite memories is of taking my father to visit Chief Robert in Big Bay. When we arrived in his village, the chief was wearing a pair of cowboy boots, a bright-red floral loincloth, mirrored sunglasses, and a blue cowboy hat. It was priceless. The custom women wear *lif nanggaria*. The nanggaria leaves are a couple of inches wide and about two feet long. To wear them, the ladies tie a vine around their waist and hang one cluster of nanggaria leaves in the front and another cluster of leaves in the back. They cover next to nothing.

On the island of Pentecost, the custom women wear what most Americans would consider to be the traditional island grass skirt, so from the waist down, they are very modest. The custom men, however, wear a *nambas*, a bit of woven pandanas mat that basically covers the point of circumcision and little more. Everything else is allowed to be fully exposed. It is not a pretty picture.

On the island of Tanna, the custom women wear grass skirts, but theirs are brilliantly colored. The custom men dress in a variety of ways, but most go *parpar*. They tie a sarong about knee length and fasten the length of it into a knot in front of them. They arrange this knot so that the length of the sarong hangs down in front of them, often dragging the ground.

On Tanna, when a man enters a village or town parpar, it is a symbol. It says something: it says, "You may have forsaken the old gods to follow this new religion, but I haven't. I have been true to the gods of my ancestors." If we were to express it in American terms, we might say that he sang with Frank Sinatra, "I did it my way."

During a church-planting crusade in the village of Irawangan, Samnalikan, a well-known custom chief, accepted Christ and decided to be baptized. When I baptized Samnalikan, he was parpar. After his baptism, he found a place to change his clothes and replaced his traditional wrap with pants and a shirt. He returned to the stream where I was baptizing other new converts and held up his sarong for all to see. He called out with a loud voice, "This is the old Samnalikan." He then grasped his shirt between his thumb and his forefinger and continued: "And this is the new Samnalikan."

I ran into his pastor a few months later in the capital city of Port Vila. I asked him, "Pastor, is Samnalikan still serving God?"

He laughed. "Missionary, he moved in with me. Every morning he insists we have devotions at five o'clock. People come from all over the island to see if it's true. 'Did Samnalikan really become a Christian?' When they come in, the first thing he does is go over to the shelf where his old sarong is lying folded up. He pulls it off the shelf, unfurls it for all to see, and declares, 'This is the old Samnalikan. This is the new Samnalikan!'"

2 Corinthians 5:17 "...if any man be in Christ, he is a new creature..."

George

George is a small trim block of a man, short, solidly muscled, and without a trace of softness. To me he looks as if he had been hewn out of the native stone of Espiritu Santo, his home island. His hands are a pair of compact, meaty squares: wide flat calloused palms, short stubby fingers, thick mud-stained fingernails.

His feet, rarely bothered by the presence of encumbering shoes, are small rectangular blocks nearly as wide as they are long. His toes are insignificant appendages compared to the bulk of the solid slab of foot. The bright pink of the nail encasing each toe provides a sharp contrast to the deep earthen brown of the rest of his feet. A thickly calloused sole wraps itself protectively around the flat base of each foot and bears the scars of thousands of treks through stone-covered river valleys and over rugged mountains. Around his ankles, the skin is cracked and broken in a series of crisscrossing lines with thick white petals peeling away from the raw inner layer, where a persistent, deep fungal infection betrays the fact that George lives in a swamp.

George may be built like a stone—solid, compact, and square; however, he is by far the most animated person I have ever met. When you first meet George, you are drawn in by a face that literally explodes with life. His smile engulfs his entire face; the deeply furrowed brow arches upward, his eyebrows shoot up in almost comic proportions and his eyes—bright, quick, intelligent eyes—dance and sparkle at the prospect of seeing an old friend or meeting a new one. But the animation doesn't end with the face; his head tilts, his entire body shifts in a way that says, "You have my fully devoted attention. Right now you are the most important thing in my world!" Don't expect him to hold that pose; George is in constant motion. His whole life is a passionate dance.

I have never met another person whose face is as expressive as George's. One of his favorite expressions is a slack-jawed look of amazement. He clings to your every word, dancing eyes wide, mouth agape as if your every sentence is a fascinating tale. He punctuates his amazed gaze with low whistles or emphatic ejaculations of "Tru! Tru!" to display his agreement or astonishment at your comments. On anyone else, such an expression would seem insincere, even mocking. But George is the kind of man that can make a bore feel entertaining. I have never seen him dismiss anyone with his glance. Everyone from respected leaders to local children receives the same undivided attention.

Bubbling beneath the surface of that compact form is a song and a dance. Watch him trekking through the jungle from one village to another, running down a stony beach to help land a boat in the breaking surf, crossing a river with medical supplies for Hope Clinic balanced on his head, splitting coconuts to feed his pigs, and as you watch him, you will see his feet shuffle and hands skip to a dance only he knows, a dance straining to burst into the open.

Repeatedly the thin veneer constraining the dance will burst. What causes these ruptures? A bend in the river, a familiar stone, the flight of a lorikeet, a jumping fish, the memory of an ancient story, the dance of life that surrounds him. There on the path, George will suddenly stop, lay down his burden, and dance. His feet move in small shuffling steps, his body sways back and forth as his weight shifts from side to side, and a deep guttural chant forms in his gut, echoes in his chest, and spills out into the world around him.

Born high in the misty cloud-cloaked mountains of Espiritu Santo, George is part of the Tiali tribe. His homeland is rugged mountains perpetually wrapped in clouds and covered with a blanket of tangled forest. Cold springs burst from benches of virgin stone; rippling brooks pool on the cusp of high mountain valleys and then leap through a fog of spray over racing cascades. Here miniature thatch huts cluster in small clearings atop high ridges, lush gardens hang precariously on the steep hillsides, old men carrying firewood on stooped backs laboriously make their way up steep muddy paths, and children race through grass-covered dales with their clear, bright laughter echoing off the face of the mountains.

This is George's world. His mother birthed him in the open *nasara* in the middle of the village over a bed of *lap lap* leaves. His father buried his dried cord in a dense grove of banana trees to perpetually tie him to the land. As a child, he ran screaming with laughter through the dales, toiling with his mother in the gardens through the day, laughing with his cousins as they swam in the cool mountain streams each evening, and, every twilight, growing drowsy to the sound of an old man's voice weaving tales as he gazed into the flickering fire at the center of their hut.

George is most adept in this world. Watch him as he strides effortlessly through the jungle. A familiar plant will make him pause along the path as he gathers its fronds to add to the evening meal. An innocuous ripple in a small mountain stream will cause him to pounce with his bush knife and triumphantly display a fish. When he senses you are tired, he will stop beside a small palm tree and cut out its heart for you to taste, patiently instructing you how to survive in his world as you rest. He will point out which vines will yield water that is safe to drink when you cut them. I have even had him explain to me in great detail how to make a poison arrow from the heart of a black palm.

George has been my guide since I first ventured into the rugged heart of Espiritu Santo. Now his hair is thoroughly sprinkled with gray, and he prefers to send his sons to guide me.

In my mind's eye, I will always see him at a bend in the mighty Ora River. On the far side of the river, an imposing stone bluff soars above us. Before us, in a wide sweep, the river stumbles down a cataract. Here on the near side, George is perched on a flat sandstone boulder. He is beating out a steady tattoo with his walking stick, weaving back and forth as wide bare feet shuffle and scrape across the surface of stone, singing the song of his world.

A Misunderstood Kindness

Wet best describes southeast Tanna. Water drizzles steadily from a leaden sky. The trees collect the fine mist and condense it into cold heavy drops. The thick undergrowth of vines, bushes, and broad leaves of banana and *lap lap* plants catches these drops and channels them in rivulets down to the muddy ground, which is carpeted in a thick layer of soggy rotten leaves.

In the midst of this sodden scene stands a small lean-to. Four sturdy posts are planted firmly in the muddy soil. Branches rudely cut to size with a machete and tied to the posts form the rafters. Palm fronds draped in numerous layers over the rafters create a thick mesh which channels most of the drizzle away and creates an almost-dry shelter under the lean-to. Centered under the lean-to, a small fire smokes as it struggles to burn wet wood and bring the water in an ash-incrusted kettle to a boil.

An old man squats just outside the smoke, his back braced against one of the posts. A close-cropped cap of graying hair covers his head. Deep creases mark his forehead and cheeks. A day's worth of thick gray stubble lines his jaws. Tattered, muddy clothes cover his sinewy arms and legs. His quick brown eyes dart back and forth between the faces of his companions. Even though his squatting body remains perfectly still, the intelligent eyes and animated face project an aura crackling with energy.

His right hand holds a thick chunk of steaming taro root, and his left waves a branch of a pepper plant. The branch of a pepper plant sports light-green oval leaves and a collection of brilliantly hot peppers ranging from pale green to deep red, tiny cone-shaped peppers that pack a powerful punch. He bites into the taro, moves the branch of peppers to his mouth, and plucks two of them with his teeth.

The old man is engaged in an animated lecture. The mouthful of taro and pepper doesn't slow him down. He continues with his mouth open wide, words slurred by thick chunks of half-chewed taro. As he speaks, widely spaced yellow teeth wobble freely in their sockets. I like the old man, I respect him, but I find it difficult to watch him talk and eat. His words trouble me more. "You see? This is just what Jon said would happen."

Tanna is a complex place. It is a small, densely populated island in the southern part of Vanuatu. The west is dry and dusty, the east wet and dripping. The north is defined by high limestone cliffs topped with a heavy layer of thick red clay; the defining feature of the south is Mount Yasur, an active volcano that constantly coats the ground with fine ash. There are only five local languages on Tanna, but the people divide themselves into 115 tribes.

Religion is even more complicated. The traditional religion of Tanna views the spiritual and physical realms as indistinguishable. Religious expression focuses primarily around manipulating the spirits to produce the desired physical results and involves incantations in forgotten or secret languages, sacred stones believed to manipulate everything from fruit trees to the weather, and wizards who specialize in interpreting the rumblings of the volcano. To this was added various expressions of Christianity and cults: Presbyterianism, Catholicism, Pentecostalism, competing Baptist churches, Mormonism, Jehovah's Witnesses, Baha'ism, and a dozen home-grown denominations/cults (sometimes it is nearly impossible to distinguish between the two).

However, the most amazing religion practiced on Tanna is the Jon Frum Cargo Cult. This cult sprang up following World War II. It focuses on material blessings. In the villages of Tanna, Jon is revered as a prophet. He is a spirit that appears and prophesies of coming wealth and prosperity. Who is Jon? Where did he come from? This is where it gets confusing. Some insist that Jon came from America, left after the war, and will one day return with everything that everyone wants. Others insist that Jon is a spirit, was on Tanna before the Americans came, and is still there speaking to men today.

Worship for Jon Frum devotees involves replicating the US troops in WWII. Hand-sewn flags and khaki uniforms, mock runways equipped with handcrafted wooden planes, and first aid posts adorned with a red cross are just a few of the colorful ways they attempt to mimic US troops. Why would they do such things?

When the initial troops arrived on Tanna, they were few in number; they carved out a rough airstrip, set up a radio shack, and strung up an American flag, and planes began to appear. The planes brought more cargo than the locals had ever seen. Clearly, those initial troops were onto a powerful form of magic. Surely, the locals reason, if they can get the mechanics right, the same blessings of cargo will flow to them.

Missionaries have long struggled with how to reach the followers of Jon with the gospel. Built into their religion is a reverence for all things American, so American missionaries find a ready audience with them. In fact, more than one passing American evangelist has claimed to have converted them. However, the evangelists come and go; Jon remains.

The followers of Jon tend to live in abject poverty. Why work? Jon is coming. He will bring you a new truck, new clothes, a new house with a TV. Why build a real medical clinic? When Jon comes, he is coming with a new medicine that will take away all sickness. Why go to school? When Jon comes, he will teach you everything you need to know in just two weeks!

Given the poverty and lack of access to medical care, many well-meaning missionaries have showered the followers of Jon with medical and other material aid. This is one of the thorniest issues in missions: compassion ministries.

Compassion is a natural fruit of knowing Christ. Christians are compassionate. It is the use of compassion in missions that gets sticky. Some argue for a no-strings-attached form of compassion. They state that Christians should do good for others just because they are Christians. They reason that acts of compassion are all the witness the lost need, that if we show compassion to others, they will understand our actions as being motivated by the love of Christ and will, in turn, want to know him.

The truth is, each of us creates our own narrative to interpret the events of our lives and especially the actions of others. The confusion comes when we assume that others are operating in the same narrative. To the American missionaries, they give to the followers of Jon to display the love of Christ, sure that if the followers know how much Christ loves them, then they will turn from Jon to Christ. Thus, to prove the love of Christ, the missionaries pour ever-increasing amounts of material aid into Tanna.

The old man was operating in a different narrative, one that explains why ever-increasing humanitarian outreaches have little to no long-term impact. He enthusiastically recounted for me all the blessings that had come to his community. To him this was solid proof that Jon, not Christ, was the true way. "You see? This is just what Jon said would happen."

Should Christians engage in compassion ministries? Yes, but before we do, we need to understand how our actions will be perceived by others. Sometimes less is more.

Acts of compassion must be accompanied by words of truth. Compassion may display love, but only truth will set you free.

Unsolicited Natanggura

This is not how I normally dress for a pastors' meeting. Today I am in cement-splattered work pants and a faded, discolored shirt. At Sanma Bible Training Center, we are in the middle of a large pour. Pouring concrete in Vanuatu is a bit different than you might expect. There is no Redi-Mix truck. Pouring concrete means hauling water, shoveling sand and coral into the mixer, pushing heavy wheelbarrows, and shutting your eyes tightly while throwing half bags of cement into the mix because the blowback will coat you in a fine gray film.

The day before, Pastor Dick, the local presbyter, asked me to drop by the pastors' meeting for a few minutes. "The pastors need an update," he insisted. I ruefully suggested that they hold the pastors' meeting at the school, and then everyone could help pour concrete and get a firsthand update. He laughed, promised to come and help more in the future, and reiterated his desire for me to brief the pastors on the progress at the school.

After apologizing for my appearance, I launched into a detailed description of the state of the work. For roofing I was using *natanggura*, a thatch made from the leaves of the sago palm. When I informed the pastors that I was purchasing my natanggura from the island of Tutuba, the entire room collectively sucked in their breath. The people on Tutuba are Presbyterian; would the missionary really buy his natanggura from Presbyterians?

Pastor Tari, a pastor from Malo, waved his hand to get my attention. His face had a strained, almost painful look. "Missionary, after you asked us for a price, my village prepared one thousand lengths of natanggura for you. Please clarify for me. Are you saying you are not going to buy them?" He clearly dreaded the idea of returning to the village and telling his members that their weeks of work had been in vain.

For a moment, I was speechless. I began to explain how by purchasing on Tutuba, I was saving significantly both on the cost of each length and on transportation. While I was talking, my mind was reeling: Had I said anything to Pastor Tari that would lead a reasonable person to conclude I was going to purchase from him?

Pastor Taki, a neighboring pastor, interrupted my explanations. "Missionary, we don't care about the price. We just want to know if you are going to buy from the Malo churches."

Welcome to trade in Vanuatu. Western concepts of trade revolve around acquiring wealth or commodities. A good trade is one that benefits both parties. One party receives the goods they seek, the other party receives remuneration. Melanesian concepts are quite different. The goal of trade in Vanuatu is developing and maintaining relationships.

In Western trade, a good buy is one where you pay the smallest possible price for the goods you need. In contrast, a good sell creates the largest possible long-term profit. We initiate trades to secure either goods or money. We buy only what we need or want. Sellers make every effort to market their products as necessary or highly desirable.

Ni-Vanuatu will purchase items that they have growing in their own garden or can secure readily from the environment, not because they need more but because they seek to initiate a relationship. Their idea of a good sell or buy is one that builds a bond between the two parties.

Ni-Vanuatu regularly enter into long-term nebulous "contracts" where one party takes something of significant value in return for a payment of an unspecified amount at an undefined point in the future. Why? To create an obligation that will lead to greater community cohesion. You don't offend someone with whom you have a large unstructured debt; if you do, they might just call it.

Unfulfilled obligations create tension in Western culture. We avoid borrowing from friends or family in order to avoid the unspoken strain that fills the air every time we meet our creditor. We would much prefer our debts to be with a faceless corporation.

In Melanesian culture, the preference is to be in debt to one's family and close friends. Neither party is in a rush for the debt to be repaid, because it functions as a security against a breach of relationship. After all, only a fool would exasperate his debtor, who might just never pay him back.

Can such a system work? Sure, especially in a context that grants status to people who disperse wealth rather than accumulate it. In spite of a slow creep toward materialism, this system has served Ni-Vanuatu well for thousands of years. Vanuatu is a host to what is termed *affluent poverty*. While few are getting rich, no one lacks food, housing, or clothing.

It is in the meshing of the two systems where conflict occurs. As a Western missionary holding church funds in a fiduciary capacity, I felt obligated to manage those funds in a responsible manner. I sought numerous quotes for the materials and, balancing the issues of cost and quality, chose my supplier.

However, as a Ni-Vanuatu, Pastor Tari made the logical presumption that I would want to strengthen the relationship between myself and his church members. Why else would I have asked for a quote? The point Pastor Taki was making in Pastor Tari's defense was that price was irrelevant. They would sell the natanggura lengths for whatever price necessary. I should be willing to bear any extra transportation costs. The money was secondary; it was the relationship that mattered.

Even after sixteen years in Vanuatu, I am occasionally caught flat-footed on cultural issues. I glanced at Pastor Dick; he was grinning. He had invited me here today to arrange this confrontation. He entered the conversation, explaining, "The missionary is purchasing *some* of his natanggura from Tutuba. Right, missionary?"

"Of course," I replied. "Everyone knows that the best natanggura comes from Malo!"

An Empty House

I sort through the heavy ring of keys, looking for one to match the padlock before me. Finding a plausible-looking one, I push it into the rusty hole. It turns roughly, grinding past the grit and rust of years of disuse. The lock pops open; I take a deep breath, pull the door open, and step inside. The house, though abandoned for years, is snug and tight. There have been no leaks, no broken windows, no vandalism.

Dust lies heavy on every surface; thousands of dead bugs—cockroaches, moths, flies, dirt daubers, and centipedes—lie scattered across the smooth cement floor. I am the first person to step into this house in nearly four years. I step hesitantly into the long narrow covered porch. Immediately before me sits a small wooden table accompanied by simple bamboo stools and a long low bench.

The doors to the house itself are locked as well. I step to the living room entrance and consult the thick ring of keys again. Inside the living room, the furniture is unmoved: a yellow love seat purchased at a yard sale, a coffee table made from a single slab of rosewood, a simple cushionless wooden bench, and a rough bookshelf empty of books. A mirror hangs on the ebony-paneled wall, patiently reflecting an empty room.

The door to the single bedroom is ajar, held open by a small black stone. A canopied queen bed is draped in its mosquito net. Across the room, the chifforobe stands open and mostly empty. A few towels, a lumpy pillow, and some odds and ends sit on its shelves. The en suite bathroom looks bare, with its curtainless shower, though the toilet still has a full bowl of water and the obligatory paper still hangs on the roller.

I backtrack to the living room and open the door to the kitchen. The kerosene fridge and the propane stove sit still and quiet. The counter top and sink are clean other than the dust and bugs that have accumulated. An empty trash can hosts several lizard skeletons. I pity the creatures that fell into the plastic deathtrap. Out of habit, I open the door to the fridge and stare at its empty shelves. I find myself opening cabinet doors and drawers and exclaiming over the utensils, dinnerware, and cookware, all neatly put away.

I walk through the house again, sit on the couch, examine the ceiling for signs of water damage, inspect the windows for signs of breakage, check the fly screen, all the while ignoring the gnawing sensations that continue to build in my heart. I hate an empty house.

This house, the first house I ever built, represents six months of my life, $25,000, weeks of patient work on a sawmill, hundreds of trips to the beach for sand and gravel, and countless trips up and down the nearby hill, lugging five-gallon jerry cans of water from the spring at its base. I admit to being a little proud: proud of its neat and tidy design, proud that it has weathered countless earthquakes and a dozen hurricanes without damage.

While building this house, I slept on the floor of the local church, bathed in the river, dealt with the stench of an outhouse, missed my family, and prayed myself to sleep each night, asking God for the funds to finish and to send a missionary to live here.

God answered my prayers. People I had never met heard about my efforts and raised the money on my behalf. The Holy Spirit used an article in the *Pentecostal Evangel* to grip the hearts of a young nurse and his wife, Brandon and Vicki Forester. He told me later that after reading the article, he wept for days. They were the first of three missionary couples that would live here. They were followed by Gary and Priscilla Ross, who gave the final three years of their missionary career, and Steven and Kara Jeager, who literally started their marriage here.

While living here, these couples ran Hope Clinic, a compassion outreach to the Tiali tribe. At the time we built here, the Tiali were the largest unreached tribe on Santo, with no evangelical churches among them. The objective of Hope Clinic was to open a door for the presentation of the gospel through a tangible expression of Christ's love.

Each of the missionary families that ministered here did their part. They stitched up the victims of domestic violence, delivered babies, treated young people for STDs, cared for an endless stream of malaria patients, and gave out thousands of doses of worming medicines. They patiently presented the gospel over and over, assisted in creating gospel recordings in the Tiali language, preached hundreds of sermons, and counseled both their patients and the budding Christian leaders in the community.

Today there is a strong church in the community. Tiali leaders preach each Sunday, govern the church's affairs, and interact with the larger body of Christ in Vanuatu. Two couples from the Tiali tribe have applied to attend Sanma Bible Training Center next year. Through the eyes of faith, I gaze just beyond the visible horizon. I see a local church reaching critical mass and engaging in the first indigenous evangelism of their own people. This is truly the ultimate goal of missions, the best possible outcome.

Yet as I sit in the dusty living room, I can't help but wonder, is God really through with this house? I know that there are seasons in ministry, that expressions of ministry are not supposed to last forever. Still, this house vibrates with memories for me: prayer meetings around that table, strategy sessions in the living room, precious interactions with new believers on the long low covered porch. I whisper my query in prayer: "God, are we done here?"

Deep in my spirit, I am sure that he answers with a quiet no. So today I posted an opening for a registered nurse or nurse practitioner at http:// wideopenmissions.org. Pray with me for the Holy Spirit to call one more missionary to serve here. Then it will be an empty house no longer.

Sun Shine

How long does it take to change eternity?

In Sun Ward's case, it was just a few weeks. Missions is, by its very nature, a long-term endeavor. There are languages to learn, cultures to master, and relationships to build prior to effective ministry. However, by partnering with a long-term missionary and a strong local church, short-term missionaries can change lives, communities, and even a nation for eternity.

Sun came to Vanuatu to explore the potential for future ministry. She had faithfully served in the Pacific in various countries for five years. The pressing question was, "Where next?" A few weeks in Vanuatu were intended to offer time for exploration of future possibilities, not aimed at changing eternity, but that is exactly what happened.

Shortly after Sun arrived, she was invited to accompany a local pastor and his children's ministry team to the island of Malo. Sun's dynamic personality and obvious love for children made her a magnet for kids and parents alike. In every village, crowds swarmed her and the ministry team, laughing at the antics of the puppets, listening attentively to the Bible stories, and responding to the altar calls.

Pastor Taki, the Assembly of God leader for the island of Malo, decided to leverage the attraction Sun provided to open a new community to the gospel. A neighboring village an hour away had been the prayer focus of his church for months. He convinced Sun to stay on Malo a few extra days in order to minister in this village. Sun's ministry proved to be the key needed to open the door to a new church plant in a community that had never had a church before.

In the few weeks Sun was in Vanuatu, she impacted the life of everyone she came in contact with. Taxi rides were prime evangelism opportunities that on at least one occasion ended with the taxi driver pouring out the brokenness of his life to Sun, who in turn led him in a sinner's prayer.

After attending a luncheon where Renee introduced her to local women, God gave her favor with key women in positions of influence in the government, business, other denominations, and the local women's center.

Using the relationships God gave her, Sun began holding weekly Bible studies on the Baptism in the Holy Spirit. The first person to receive the Baptism in the Holy Spirit was the son of a prominent business owner; the second was the wife of the Anglican bishop! Rather than feeling threatened, the bishop requested a meeting with Sun and extended an invitation for her to preach for three nights on the Baptism in the Holy Spirit to all of the Anglican leaders at the central Anglican church!

In four months, Sun was instrumental in a new church plant, led numerous people to make a decision for Jesus, prayed the wife of an Anglican bishop and others through to the Baptism in the Holy Spirit, and spent three nights preaching to Anglican leaders about the Baptism. Sun's experience shows that short-term missionaries can change eternity.

How long does it take to change eternity? In the case of Sun Ward, about sixteen weeks.

The Lady in Black

Port Resolution is a beautiful place. The crescent-shaped bay is lined with a black sandy beach. The headlands of the bay are towering red cliffs standing high above crashing waves. A gentle stream bisects the beach, its cool water creating a rippled pattern in the sand over a large delta that extends out into the bay only a few inches below sea level. On the eastern side of the bay, hot springs bubble up through the sand and fill ocean-side pools with scalding water.

The road to Port Resolution takes you down a hill before entering a long U-shaped coastal plain. At the bottom of the hill, there is a large banyan tree on the right-hand side of the road. This banyan, more than 250 years old, once stood on the seaside. This tree, now more than two miles from the coast, is the tree that the first missionary to Tanna tied his boat to when he came ashore.

The road goes beyond the hill and begins to cross the coastal plain. Is it a product of volcanic uplift or just silt from the river that bisects it? It is an open question. Mount Yasur, a very active volcano less than ten miles away, could be causing considerable uplift, but it also spews enormous amounts of ash that, carried by the river, could easily be silting up the bay.

The coastal plain is filled with the dense brush of guava trees. As you approach the coast, the brush gives way to a large, open, park-like green. Framed by the river, the mountains, and the thick guava brush, this green contains a small unnamed village. Guarding the entrance to the beach are enormous carvings of local deities. The wood they are carved from has bleached in the sun to a light gray. They are decorated with an abundance of vibrant tropical flowers. The rich colors of the flowers and the dull gray of the wood would make a beautiful contrast if it were not for their purpose.

I am here for a very simple reason: we need sand. While sand from the beach is not a good choice for building, on Tanna it is the only option. Since we are pouring the foundation for the church at Iatapu, we need sand. This is the nearest.

After we load the truck with sand, I stay behind to stroll the beach. The truck will return soon for a second trip, so I have a little time to explore. I make my way over to the steaming pools of water that bubble up from beneath the sand. They have stained the rocks with a rainbow of colors ranging from rich rusty red to sulfur yellow. I dip my finger in a pool and yank it back, shocked at the heat. Later I learn that locals cook here on a daily basis.

Just up the beach from the hot springs, I see a woman wearing a Mother Hubbard dress walking toward me. Mother Hubbard dresses were designed by the early missionaries to give the local women a modest form of clothing. Since the pre-Christian form of clothing in Vanuatu is a matter of a few strategically placed leaves, some reform was clearly needed. The result was a large blousy dress that is fairly constant throughout the Pacific and, in Vanuatu, is referred to as an island dress.

The trademark of an island dress is bright floral patterns and lots of lace and ribbons. Local women love these dresses and wear them at any special occasion. Men must love them too, as one of the most popular songs in Vanuatu is titled "Island Dress Blong MI!" and features a man singing about how he loves to see his sweetheart in an island dress.

The stunning thing about this woman's island dress is its color, or rather its lack thereof. It is as black as the sand I am standing on, blacker really, more like the black of the ash from Mount Yasur. I assume that she is in mourning. When she reaches me, we begin to discuss the beauty of the beach and the amazing heat of the hot springs. She offers to cook some food for me in the spring for a small fee, but I decline. I try to avoid any appearance of being a tourist since Ni-Vanuatu tend to have a pretty low opinion of tourists. So instead, we stand on the beach and talk.

I soon discover that she is a member of the Jon Frum Cargo Cult. This cult believes that by properly imitating the uniforms, buildings, marching drills, and flag of the United States Army, they can tap into the mystical supply of wealth that Americans enjoy. A few years back, a prophet arose in this cult; his name is Fred. Fred is a leper, and his disfigured appearance may help convince his followers that he has a connection to the spirit world.

Fred has deified Mount Yasur and added this belief to the cult. He claims the volcano speaks to him in its eruptions and that only he can interpret its words. Fred has a significant following, no doubt due to the fact that he has made some stunning prophesies that have come true. I ask if her island dress means that she is in mourning. "No, no," she explains, "the volcano spoke to Fred. It told him I should wear only black; it represents the earth."

My new friend is a fervent follower of Fred. She tells me that all she really wants is to enjoy the same standard of living that Americans have. If she just had more money and more things, then everything would be all right. How tragic.

The same lie of Satan that has Americans running after things, abandoning their families, and forsaking God is at work here. Gently I expose the lie for what it is: a mirage, a shifting shadow, an illusion that beckons but never fulfills. "Things and money can never satisfy," I promise. "Only God can." I run into stiff resistance. She is invested too heavily in this deception to give it up easily.

I don't know her name, but I pray for the lady in black.

What If?

Daydream with me for a bit.

What if every person in your home town became a Christian tomorrow? Imagine next Sunday: policemen directing traffic at the entrances to church parking lots, long lines outside church doors, cars weaving their way up and down the lanes in church parking lots, vainly looking for a spot close to the door.

Imagine the church services: new converts eager to make a public declaration of their faith, pastors overwhelmed by the influx of new faces, Sunday School rooms bursting with rowdy kids, families rejoicing that their lost loved ones have come to Christ, tears streaming down the faces of saints that have prayed for revival their entire lives. Wouldn't it be wonderful?

Let's dream bigger. Let's imagine that everywhere around the world, in every city, town, and hamlet where there is a church, any kind of church, tomorrow every person makes the decision to follow Christ. It would be a global news event.

The world would be transformed. Overnight many wars would cease, peace would break out, brothels would be closed, sex slaves freed, hungry people fed, the homeless given shelter, the bars and nightclubs transformed to churches. In a single day, billions would come to know Christ. It would truly be awesome!

The tragedy? Half of the people that are lost without Christ today would still be without him then. In a world of seven billion people, two billion claim to be Christians. Of the remaining five billion, half live in a town or community where there is a Christian who can tell them about Christ. Two and a half billion people live in communities where there are no churches, there are no Christians, and no one is coming to tell them about Jesus tomorrow, because in their community, there is no light.

It was a typical American restaurant: real plates and silverware, crisp white tablecloth, nice lighting, clean environment. The waitstaff were cleanly dressed and attentive, the salad bar filled with fresh, inviting salads. An enormous menu described delicious entrees. The low roar of friendly chatter was punctuated by the occasional clink and clatter as tables were cleared of dishes. The pastor seated across from me was a rather typical American as well: midfifties, heavy, balding, with drops of sweat breaking out on his high forehead in spite of the air conditioning. I could tell he was having a hard time getting to what he wanted to say—never good news for a missionary.

He began by explaining that the church had suffered a reversal. Income was down significantly. Families had found it necessary to move out of town in order to find work. The family that had initially supported our ministry had moved. Frankly, the church didn't have the funds to pay a missions pledge initiated at the behest of a former member. I could tell he was uncomfortable and regretted the need for this conversation. I tried to ease the situation by assuring him that I understood completely. I didn't blame him.

I asked if I could visit the church, present our ministry again, and see if perhaps the current members would increase their missions giving. His reply stunned me. "I know that people overseas have needs, but the truth is, we have needs right here in this community. I can't begin to meet all the needs right here at home. If I can't meet the needs in my own community, why would I give money to missions?"

I sat back in my chair, almost too stunned for words. Why? Because missions is not about meeting needs. I place the blame for this misconception squarely on the shoulders of missionaries. For a million reasons, some of them good, missionaries have used the poverty of the majority of the world to motivate Western Christians to give. Poverty is not the problem. Spiritual darkness is the problem.

There is poverty at home. Why should you neglect the hungry child next door to buy a meal for a hungry child across the seas? You shouldn't.

Christian love is best displayed to one's neighbor. If missions was about feeding the hungry, then I would urge you to feed your neighbor first, then those overseas. But missions is not about feeding the hungry.

Missions is not about feeding the hungry, providing medical care, drilling wells to provide clean water, rescuing children trapped in prostitution—though sometimes missionaries need to do these things. Missions is not about building churches, raising literacy, printing Bibles, education or Bible schools—though sometimes missionaries must do these things and a thousand others. Missions is about getting the gospel to those who have no realistic expectation of hearing it unless someone crosses a linguistic and cultural barrier to present Christ to them.

The church has myriad ministries. All of them are valid. The church has a responsibility to evangelize. You and your church have a mandate to passionately pursue every lost person in your community. In fact, the church must seek out the lost wherever they are. You and your church have a mandate to display the love of Christ to the hurting. That should take a physical form in your community. When we do these things collectively, we sometimes call it missions. That's okay, as long as we don't obscure the core issue.

I am not attempting to devalue any expression of ministry; all are important. I am saying there is that which is core to missions and that which is not. That which is not core to missions seeks to win those who have the opportunity to hear but have yet to respond. Is this valid? Vital? Yes.

However, missions, at its core, endeavors to take the gospel to those who have no opportunity to hear. It seems to me that we must clearly define the core of missions and that once it is clearly defined, it must be given priority.

In a village in Pakistan, Afghanistan, Mongolia, China, North Korea, Tibet, Cambodia, Egypt, Chad, Vanuatu, or a thousand other places, an old man pokes his fire and mumbles at the darkness. His limbs are tired and worn. His skin drapes loosely over ribs too clearly seen. He struggles to pull shallow breaths and moves slowly and painfully. Red-rimmed eyes peer out underneath craggy eyebrows. Amulets, tokens of religion, surround him. Still he fears the unseen; he fingers a juju hung around his neck; he anticipates that soon he will slip into the spirit world. He looks for light but finds only darkness.

I wonder: If everyone does what you do, will he hear of Christ before it is too late?

The Sons of Cannibals

For a split second time stands still. The sun beats down relentlessly. The rhythmic scrape of shovels pauses. Surprised silence throbs in my ears. Dust hangs motionless in the hot still air. The men of Leviamp, spill out of the truck before me. The men of Vinmavis, each cradling a pick, shovel or bush knife halt behind me. I stand between the sons of cannibals. Two villages embodying generations of tribal warfare and a retaliatory cannibalism. How did I get here?

I am the first passenger off the small twin-engine plane. It is raining as I step out onto the tarmac at Norsup Airport. The raindrops splash down onto the hot asphalt and, quickly converting to vapor form again, drift upward as lazy steam. Before me are the burned-out remains of a terminal building. Endless land disputes, the bane of Vanuatu, result in this particular airport being burned and closed several times a year.

I scan the small crowd clustering around the gate to the runway; some, burdened down with small bags, boxes, and chickens, are waiting to board the plane to travel to Port Vila, others, empty-handed, are waiting to receive a friend or loved one home. No one looks even vaguely familiar. I pick my bags up off the luggage buggy, little more than a two-wheeled wheelbarrow, weave my way through the crowd to the shelter of a small section of roofing that has been reattached to the burned-out building, and hide from the rain.

The pilot motions to the passengers to board; the rain makes the fare-wells short, and the crowd thins as the travelers depart. The remnant of the crowd begins to disperse, some melting into jungle trails, others jumping into the beds of the four waiting trucks. No one moves to claim me, so I am pretty certain that I have been forgotten at the airport. I bum a ride on the last remaining truck going to Lakatoro.

Lakatoro, while not incorporated, is *the* town for Malakula. Malakula has two claims to fame: one, it is home to two of Vanuatu's most famous tribes, the Big Nambas and the Small Nambas—interesting names, given what *nambas* means. The other is that it has the most recent history of can-nibalism in Vanuatu.

Once an anthropologist explained to me that there really had never been any cannibalism in Vanuatu. It was just a myth, he explained, created by missionaries who needed the Ni-Vanuatu to be really savage in order to increase their fund-raising potential.

One writer explained that the Ni-Vanuatu had practiced cannibalism but that it had been a carefully crafted system and that it was very "sus-tainable." I had to laugh: sustainable for whom? I bet it didn't feel very sustainable if you were the one in the cooking pot! I am sure it didn't seem sustainable to the mother, father, children, or spouse of the victim.

It is easy to explain away cannibalism from the air-conditioned lounge of a hotel in Port Vila; here in Malakula, you meet ground truth. I have met men who freely admit that they have eaten human flesh. I asked one, an old man by the name of Arnold from the Big Nambas tribe, how many victims he had eaten. He shrugged his shoulders and told me he hadn't counted; "It was just meat," he said. In 1968 the last public cannibal feast was held by the Big Nambas tribe. As late as the last decade, men have been tried and convicted of killing and eating the victims of ritual cannibalism.

The man I am expecting to meet me at the airport, Pastor Lester, is the son of a cannibal. His father is famous in the Big Nambas tribe for kill-ing two men in one day and bringing them back to the village for supper. Today Pastor Lester is the senior pastor of the Assembly of God church in Leviamp village and the presbyter for Malampa District of the Assemblies of God. Had the gospel not come to Malakula, he might have followed in his father's steps as a warrior and eater of the dead. Instead, he is a peace-maker, one who brings the light of eternal life to darkened villages.

I have come to Lakatoro to help Pastor Lester build a church. The local leadership has targeted Lakatoro as the site for their next church plant. Evangelism started last year, a small cell of believers has been established, and they believe this year a church will be born. The building will serve several purposes: it will be a home for the fledgling church, a Bible training center for training future pastors, and a district office for the Malampa Province of the Assembly of God.

Early the next morning, Pastor Lester meets me on the grounds for the new building, and he apologizes for not meeting me at the airport. His jaw is swollen, and he is clearly in pain; "my teeth" is his two-word explanation. There is no dentist on Malakula, so decaying teeth leave people in agony for weeks. Someone else was supposed to come in his stead, he explains, but he gave them the wrong flight time. I tell him to forget about it, and we set about laying out the building.

Yesterday's rain is a distant memory, the sun beats down with a glaring intensity, and by eight, the heat is rapidly building. The construction site has recently been bulldozed, and the fine soil rises in stifling clouds with each footfall. It promises to be a broiling day.

Pastor Lester and I have not completed squaring the building when the first truckload of workers arrives. They are from the village of Vinmavis, a neighboring and formerly rival village to Leviamp. We gather round for a short prayer, and then I begin to explain the size and depth of the footings we need to dig. Shortly after work commences, the second truck arrives, this one from Leviamp.

In that second of silence I wonder what happens next. Will faith and love triumph over generations of hatred? The moment passes, I hear the men greet each other with laughter, smiles, and cries of *"Epas, epas*. It is good, it is good."* Throughout the long day, they labor in the hot sun, shovels break the ground, dust flies, and sweat pours. Jokes are told, laughter is shared, and a meal enjoyed under a nearby shade tree.

One generation ago, a meeting between these two villages would have sparked bloodshed. Today, I watch as the sons of cannibals labor together to build a church.

Christian Tourism

A group of tourists sits sunburned and dazed on the sidewalk of Rue De Luganville. Like all tourists, they are dressed terribly: mismatched outfits, floppy hats, and shorts that reveal blindingly white legs. Their eyes, which stretch wide to try to take in everything, yet see only half of what is before them, give them a distinct deer-in-the-headlights look. Chaotic chatter reveals that they are thrilled by discovering the local stores have bottled water and dismayed that none of the ATMs work. Their guide arrives with a truck full of luggage and begins to round them up, herding them into waiting buses, seeking out stragglers, reassuring the concerned, and resolving petty issues. What is different about this group of tourists? They are a church group on a missions trip, and their guide is a missionary.

Before you crucify me, let me set the record straight: I do believe in short-term missions. A trip to Mexico at the age of twelve profoundly influenced my life. A survey of those serving full-time in missions will find that most participated in short-term missions before committing to a lifetime of service. Churches which regularly send short-term teams are more engaged in missions, give more for global evangelism, have more aggressive evangelism efforts in their home community, and develop and send more career missionaries. As a missionary, I have been encouraged and assisted in fulfilling my vision by great teams, but it would be naïve to disregard the pitfalls that abound.

Here are some truths about short-term missions trips that you should know: They require weeks of preparation by host missionaries, often distracting them from their core ministry. The ministry effectiveness of the team members is cut in half by the language barrier, regardless of the skill of your interpreter, and then halved again by cultural dissonance. Churches, pastors, and the individuals in the congregations where you minister often value you more as an opportunity for financial gain than for the spiritual input you seek to have in their lives. Conflicting objectives of the sending church, the individuals that make up the team, the host missionary, and the host church often leave one or more parties feeling, at best, unfulfilled and, more often than not, used.

There is also a pitfall that is common knowledge on the field but often unheard of back home. That is the missionaries that become de facto tour operators. Shortly after I arrived on the field, an independent missionary offered to show me the ropes of handling short-term missions groups. "That's what we do," he boasted. I was shocked to discover that was truly the entirety of his ministry: he hosted church groups.

As shocking as it might seem, he is not alone. Another independent missionary I know is rarely present in the country other than when he is hosting a team. He carefully shelters his team members from contact with other missionaries lest the team members ask questions that prove to have embarrassing answers. He takes them to work sites of other missionaries building schools, clinics, and churches and discusses them as if they were joint projects. Ready for the shocker? These men are highly respected by their sending churches, the best-equipped and the best-funded missionaries on the island.

How do we engage in short-term missions and avoid these pitfalls?

First, partner with a missionary who is accountable to other missionaries. It is easy for a missionary tour guide to con a pastor for two weeks, nearly impossible to con a missionary with twenty years of experience. Missions boards comprised of pastors or loved ones are rarely effective accountability partners for missionaries.

Second, come to connect with and enhance the long-term ministry strategy of the resident missionary. A seasoned missionary, fluent in the language and familiar with local culture and customs, can be your bridge to effective ministry, provide a helpful orientation once you arrive, and connect you with key ministry and government leaders.

Be objective about the amount of change that your team can bring in a two-week period. Regardless of how it may seem, people are no more pliable on the missions field than they are in your home town. Working in conjunction with a missionary who will remain behind after you leave allows your ministry to have a lasting impact.

Start your trip with realistic expectations of what you will accomplish. The most important thing that will happen on your missions trip will be what happens spiritually in the lives of those participating. The goal is that they will recognize the superficial nature of Western materialism and commit themselves in a greater measure to God and his kingdom.

The second-most important thing that will happen on your missions trip is what happens in the lives of the host missionary and their family. The goal is that they are encouraged and built up spiritually. Bear in mind that the ministry you give during this time may be the only ministry the missionary children ever hear in their own language. Ministering to the missionary family is the most significant opportunity you have for making a long-term difference in your host country.

A distant third is what actually gets done, whether it is building a church, providing medical care, or an evangelistic crusade. While this may be difficult for task-oriented Americans to accept, the reality is that regardless of your skill set, you will be impaired by the language barrier, lack of cultural understanding, and jet lag. If the task were the important thing then many times more-effective work could be accomplished if you simply sent the money spent on airfare to the missionary for him to hire local help.

If you can begin with realistic expectations and then place the emphasis on those things that matter most, you will be a long way ahead in having a successful missions trip without becoming merely Christian tourists.

Hokua Means Wind

A steel-gray mountain of water roars toward us. Its face is a complex maze of competing waves; its crest curls and breaks as it speeds toward us. The wind drives its broken tip horizontally above the surface of the ocean. The salt spray whips my clothes, stings my eyes, and fills my mouth with a bitter bite. I am too busy clinging to the side of the small aluminum boat to wipe my eyes. Through the burning lens of salt water, I watch the wave now towering thirty feet above the boat. For a moment, its menacing brow hangs in the air, suspended over the boat; then suddenly the crest collapses onto itself, and a foaming torrent of water slides down the side of the liquid mountain and slams into the boat, burying the roof and bow windows. A wall of water washes over me, Renee, our kids, and the pastors accompanying us. The boat wallows beneath the weight of the wave for a moment before bobbing to the surface.

We summit the wave, and for a moment, I see the horizon. Before us a haunting vision plays out: low dark clouds, screaming wind, mile after mile of churning, foaming surf, an endless series of massive dark swells. Beneath the small shelter at the bow, my thirteen- and seven-year-old boys, Drew and Eli, wrapped in bright-orange life vests, bounce amidst the baggage. Beside me, Bryan, my nineteen-year-old son, looks at me with frank eyes. "We're in a tight spot," he says with his characteristic understatement. Across the boat, Renee, my wife of twenty-three years, and Alecia, my twenty-one-year-old daughter, cling to the sides of the boat in exhaustion.

I scan the coastline, looking for a safe haven, and see only jagged rock faces buried in white breakers. There is no way out.

Two days earlier, I left the village of Wunpuku on the west coast of Santo in search of cell phone reception. We tooled lazily up the coast on glassy-calm indigo water. Twin fishing lines streamed out in the wake of the boat. A cheerful banter filled the air; the atmosphere was easy, relaxed. The coast was lined with massive slabs of rough gray stone, which, to an experienced eye, conveyed that this was a deadly place when the wind was wrong. Our guide pointed to a crease between the stones, indicating the entrance to our harbor.

Sliding into the groove between towering boulders, we entered the passage at Hokua. Beyond the bottleneck, the harbor opened up with breathtaking beauty. Low-growing thick scrub topped the rim of the enclosure. Beneath this green cape, its gray coral walls were lined with hand-carved canoes ready to be launched. The deep-blue depth of the ocean yielded to a wonderland of translucent blues overlaying a rich tapestry of hard and soft corals, brilliantly colored fish, creeping octopuses, and prickly sea urchins—a snorkeler's paradise.

We followed our guide up the narrow path, which twisted its way up the hillside, through the dense brush of tropical forest, past grazing cattle beneath wispy coconut palms, and into the village of Hokua. We quickly exited the village, heading north and east toward the coast on the opposite side of the peninsula. The trees transitioned to ironwood and other tough hardwoods that tolerate salt spray and endless wind. The ground beneath my feet transitioned from dark loam to sand and finally to a jumble of rough coral stones.

We broke through the thick stand of ironwood and onto the bare stones overlooking the sea. A brisk wind whistled through the branches of the trees behind us. Before me the ocean was covered with wind-whipped swells averaging six to nine feet. We sat on stony outcroppings waiting for cell phone coverage that never came. As we waited, my guide told me that the name of the village, Hokua, means "wind." "Right now," he told me, "it's okay. Just make sure that you don't try to round the point at the end of the peninsula when the wind is really blowing."

His words of warning are ringing in my ears when we set out from Wunpuku two days later. I caution the captain. I try to make it clear: with my family onboard, I don't want to take risks. "Sure, missionary," he answers. "If it's bad, we will turn around." At dawn, when we start out, the conditions are idyllic. We are still on the western, leeward side of the island. The sun is just breaking over the mountains as the boat noses into the calm waters.

As we approach the point, a rapid-fire discussion ensues in the tribal language of the captain. Though I speak Bislama, the national language of Vanuatu, fluently, there are one hundred tribal languages on Santo. Learning them is impossible. The result? Far too often I am in the dark. The pastors with me understand; the two deckhands understand. I find out later they are all begging the captain to turn back. He refuses.

I ask the pastor and captain for the verdict. "There is some tidal chop," the captain answers. "We will be careful navigating it, and then we will be home free." It is common to have a patch of rough water near points that project out from the shoreline, so his explanation sounds plausible. An hour later and we break around the point. Instead of relenting, the situation rapidly deteriorates. Beyond the point, we face the full brunt of a strong southeasterly. Massive swells dominate the horizon for as far as I can see.

Too late the captain realizes his mistake. In these seas, there is no turning around. Were we to try, the boat would capsize midturn, flipped by the wind-driven waves. The windward eastern coast, battered by the waves, offers no safe harbors and no place to hide. For hours he points the small boat into the swells, dodging the worst of the breaking waves, focusing all his efforts on avoiding a disaster. The waves pound, the wind whistles, the engine races, and the little boat valiantly struggles up mountain after mountain.

Behind the thick veil of clouds, the sun marches across the sky; time passes, but the boat makes little to no forward progress. Maintaining position and avoiding catastrophe is only a temporary solution. Soon the fuel will be finished, and so will we. My prayers all but become a mantra. I entreat for protection, I ask for calm, I beg for mercy. I plead the life of my children and my wife. No one speaks. The faces are tense and stoic. The wind continues to scream; the waves pound relentlessly. I fear it will never end.

In the moment, in the middle of the storm, it often seems God is silent, unhearing, unanswering. Psalms 107 describes God's mercy on those caught in the storm at sea. It says he brings them "unto their desired haven." His mercy is not always in the miraculous end to the storm but in the safe resolution of the journey.

Slowly, painfully slowly, the boat begins to progress against the waves. Seven hours after we start out, the boat slips behind the point of Pesena into the safe haven of Wora. There we stumble up the steep stone beach and collapse onto rich green grass beneath a massive banyan tree, exhausted but so thankful for his mercies.

In Splendor

The rain starts in the night and continues into the morning unabated. A steady drizzle soaks the ground, slowly fills puddles, worms its way through unseen pinholes in roofs, and drips incessantly from branches and eaves and through bedroom ceilings. Once every hour or so, a distant roar cuts through the steady dripping, growing in volume as it nears. The tiresome dripping is replaced with the strident, urgent sound of heavy drops slamming into leaves, tin roofs, and puddles.

The heavy drops come slowly at first, but their rate rapidly accelerates. Suddenly the roar breaks into the open. Dense leaden drops rush across the yard from the east, providing a clear line of demarcation between the drizzle and downpour. Mercilessly they crash into the ramshackle tin hut.

The puddles stretching across the yard erupt into furious gouts of muddy water at the advance of the storm. The broad, flat, lobed leaves of a breadfruit tree bob and dance under the onslaught. The tin roof of the shack quivers and shakes beneath the weight of the deluge suddenly dumped on it. Water pours off the roof, feeding into the maze of mud and puddles littering the yard. A young bride dressed in an immaculate white dress stands in the doorway and stares out at the downpour.

I pity brides in Vanuatu. If June is wedding month in America, then December is wedding month in Vanuatu. The *why* seems a bit evasive. Mostly I think it is a function of New Year's resolutions and procrastination. Marriage in Vanuatu is a family affair. A young couple doesn't simply decide to marry, set a date, and invite friends and family. In Vanuatu the extended family is deeply involved in the selection of the husband/wife, has veto power of potential matches, must agree to the date, and often causes last-minute delays and cancelations.

In January families vow that this year, they will arrange for the marriage of their children. Wedding dates are normally set for April or May, then put off till August or September. Ultimately, December arrives, and no wedding has taken place. Under pressure from their children, who want to marry, and church leaders who are concerned about common law marriages, the family finally buckles and conducts the ceremony in a rushed manner before Christmas.

If June is known for outdoor weddings garnished with perfect weather, December is its antithesis. Hurricane season rages in Vanuatu in December. When no gale force winds are blowing, stifling heat and smothering humidity are the norm. Rainless days are few and far between. Most days are marked by periods of steady drizzle broken by moments of intense downpours.

Because of the never-ending rain in December, the road maintenance crews fall hopelessly behind schedule. The back roads become an impossible collection of potholes bridged by strips of crumbling pavement. The muddy footpaths that line each side of the road are worn free of grass and host deep puddles of their own. Vigilance is required of those who trod these paths as passing trucks splash out great waves of chocolate water when their tires plunge off the narrow bits of pavement and into each puddle.

The bride stares out at the thundering rain, the maze of mud and standing water. It is time for the wedding. No car comes to carry her to the church, yet walking in this downpour is impossible. She waits, knowing that most of the wedding guests are mirroring her actions, standing just out of reach of the deluge and waiting for a break in the weather.

When the rain slackens back to a manageable pace, she begins her journey. A sister holds a broad umbrella over her. Rubber boots temporarily replace the dainty white slippers she will wear during the ceremony. She lifts the skirt and petticoats of her dress high to avoid the mud that will spring from the soles of the boots with each step.

She gingerly makes her way across the yard and down the narrow footpath lining the road. Her progress is carefully timed. She keeps a wary eye trained down the road, anticipating any passing trucks and timing their perigee so that she is not adjacent to any potholes as they pass. Her steps are slow, careful, and deliberate. Amazingly, she makes it to the churchyard unspotted.

At the churchyard, she is met with frantic signals from the front door. "Wait!" the signals say. "We're not ready yet!" So she waits. The church is a simple cinderblock building. Gaping holes in the place of windows and doors mark its rough unfinished walls. The churchyard is strewn with pits of mud and standing water. A pamplimus tree, its low, twisting branches sporting clusters of large grapefruit-like citrus fruits, dominates the middle of the churchyard.

Hanging from the branches of the pamplimus are four quarters of a freshly slaughtered beef. Blood drips from the quarters, mingling with the water and mud beneath the tree. Young men hack at the quarters with dull knives. They indiscriminately sever muscles and toss them into waiting rubber tubs. Blood and bits of fatty membrane spray out as each slab of meat is unceremoniously dumped into the tubs.

The dull roar of an impending cloudburst begins to build. The bride and her party, desperate for shelter, push underneath the thick tangle of branches of the pamplimus tree. I stand on the porch of the church and watch her there. I feel sorry for her to be placed in such circumstances on her wedding day. Yet I find myself amazed at her as well. Incredibly, in spite of the rain, the mud, the muddy path she had to walk, the impromptu butchery in the churchyard, she has kept herself and her dress spotless.

In Ephesians 5:27 Paul describes Christ's cleansing and care for the church. He says that the church will be presented "in splendor." In splendor? I have traveled all over this world; I have visited Christ's church on all six inhabited continents. I have seen the good, the bad, and the ugly. I have watched the church struggling through the mire and mud of this world. Truthfully, the word *splendor* never came to mind.

Yet Christ gave himself for the church. He has cleansed us with his Word. He calls us to navigate this muddy, messy world. Fully confident, knowing without question that his church will be presented to himself "without spot or wrinkle or any such thing, that she might be holy and without blemish."

As I look at the young bride, her garments clean and unblemished, I reflect on the path she traversed. I watch her standing next to the gore of the butchering. I see a picture of the church, Christ's bride—a church that has been cleansed yet not removed from the world. No posh limousine whisks her from door to door. No, she slogs a muddy road in the worst of circumstances. In splendor.

When the Roof Rots

I sat beside the pastor and listened incredulously as he explained that he planned to abandon his church building. I had spent thousands of dollars, weeks of my time, and the efforts of a missions team and nearly wrecked my relationship with him to get this building built. Visiting now, years later, I looked around in despair. The church building had never been improved. The yard was overgrown. The surrounding houses were abandoned and in disrepair. What had gone wrong?

Since he was a proven pastor, I readily agreed when he asked me to help him with yet another church plant. Situated at the intersection of a coastal road and a major river, this village is not a typical village. Most villages occupy traditional tribal lands and have only one language. However, over time, representatives of various tribes in the interior of Santo have migrated here to have greater access to the road. This gathering of tribes yields a village of people speaking eight different languages.

The potential for disagreements and violence in such a mixed population is significant. The chief is tasked primarily with maintaining order. He seeks to keep unity at all costs. New ways are not tolerated, creating one of the few roadside villages in Vanuatu that still primarily cling to custom and the traditional dress of *malmal* for the men and *lif nanggaria* for the women.

We began by holding Bible studies in the pastor's kitchen. At first only a few children would join us. After a few weeks, they were followed by a handful of women and some questioning men. As the crowd began to grow, it posed a threat to the tranquility of the village. It was disrupting the established order. The chief sternly warned the pastor to stop the studies, and when he refused, the warnings swiftly turned to threats of violence. The new believers fled the main village in fear and carved out a small village of their own just downstream.

A visiting evangelist passed the story to a friend in the States, who in turn passed it on to the pastor of a church with significant resources. Late one evening, I received the kind of phone call every missionary loves: "I heard about your need. We would like to help build a church in this community." A persecuted Ni-Vanuatu church, a generous American congregation, and a missionary to tie the two together—what could be better?

I passed the news on to the small group of believers. "We are part of the family of God," I told them, "a family that spans the whole world. Some of your brothers and sisters in America want to help you. They are going to pay for you to build a church." My words were met with stunned whistles of disbelief and rejoicing.

Excitement began to build. The church went through the painstaking process of securing a title to a small piece of ground. A Baptist missionary friend drew up plans for the building. A team from California volunteered to assist in the construction. I made hundreds of trips up and down the bumpy road, carrying supplies. We were all working together to build the kingdom of God. Right?

In the hurry and bustle of it all, slowly and subtly, our focus changed. No longer were we intent on weekly Bible studies to build up a group of believers. Now we were focused on building plans, staging supplies, and coordinating the efforts of the missions team. Our efforts shifted from the Church to the church.

Tension rose between the American time schedule of the missions team and the Ni-Vanuatu version of time. Rain delayed construction. Months passed. Headquarters grew impatient with the pace of the work and demanded the work be completed or the funds returned. The sponsoring church asked for pictures and progress reports.

As a missionary, I knew several things:

- Things don't happen quickly in Vanuatu.
- The church members needed to own the building through sweat equity.

- Headquarters would follow through on their threats to garnish my wages if the project reports weren't completed soon.
- The sponsoring church deserved to see timely results of their funds.

Against my better judgment, I brought in a group of pastors from another island to get the building completed. Together the pastors and I struggled to bring the church building into reality. We sweated in the sun and shivered in the rain while the church members sullenly watched from the shelter of their porches. The pastors complained about the laziness of the members, and the church members vowed that if it couldn't happen their way, then the pastors could do all the work themselves.

In the end, I *succeeded*. I was able to report to headquarters that the project was complete. I was able to take photos of a completed building to send to the sponsoring church. The sponsoring church was able to celebrate the results of their gift.

Yet by taking the responsibility for building the church building out of the hands of the church, I stunted its growth and damaged it irreparably.

This is one of the dilemmas of modern missions. Few things are more popular in America than building a church. We like tangible results. But a Church is not the building. Building a Church doesn't happen on a neat time schedule; it doesn't produce a tangible result.

When a missionary accepts money to build church buildings, it moves their focus off of the eternal and onto the temporal. When a missionary agrees to host a team to put up a church, it moves the focus off of winning souls, making disciples of new believers, and training pastors and onto staging materials for construction.

When a new church doesn't struggle to build a place of worship, it misses a vital spiritual exercise needed to build up the faith and unity of the believers.

In the end, our help often hurts.

David touches on an important principal when Araunah offered to give David oxen to make a sacrifice. David refused his gift and insisted on paying for them, saying, "Neither will I offer burnt offerings unto the Lord my God of that which doth cost me nothing." 2 Samuel 24:24 (KJV)

I will never forget the pastor's words to me that morning: "Missionary, we will worship here till the roof rots. Then it's finished."

Those are the words of a man whose offering cost him nothing.

But I Never Told
Anyone!

The phone rang late Saturday night. "Bryan, Granny Webb passed away today," my mother told me. "The funeral will be on Monday. I know it would mean a lot to your daddy if you could make it." Ten thousand miles from home, I pondered the impossibility of making such a trip on late notice. In spite of the late hour, I was able to reach the local agent for Air Pacific on his cell. "Don't worry, pastor," he told me. "We will take care of you."

The next morning, I presented myself at the local airport and quietly asked to board the morning flight to Port Vila. The agent behind the counter looked at me quizzically. "Where's your ticket?"

"No gat," I answered. "Be Bubu woman blong mi i ded. I don't have one, but my grandmother has died." There was a brief consultation behind the counter, and I was handed a boarding pass for my first ticketless leg in an amazing trip that covered over ten thousand miles and involved twenty hours of flight time. The amazing thing? I flew the entire trip from Santo to Dallas without a single ticket.

After boarding I leaned back into the narrow seat, closed my eyes, and recalled a scene from my childhood. It was pretty typical for a small Pentecostal church. It was a Wednesday-night service, the air conditioner wasn't quite up to the job, and the hand fans were working valiantly across the auditorium to try and make up the difference. The usual crowd was present with a few visitors, the most prominent of whom was a woman evangelist.

She was all of five foot tall, medium build, with brilliant white hair. Her singularly most outstanding physical characteristic was her eyes. One was blind, long ago covered over by a thick white film, the stuff of a little boy's nightmares. The remaining eye was sharp and penetrating. You could hardly stand to look in that eye, for you felt as if it were peering into the secrets of your soul.

The sermon wasn't terribly well organized. The method was what is called "Following the Spirit." The topic evolved as the sermon progressed. Sometimes it rambled a bit; other times it hit upon a topic for which this white-haired evangelist felt a great deal of passion. Thus, the volume tended to rise and fall in a pulsing rhythm. Yet all over the congregation, you could feel a tension, a spiritual anticipation rising. Everyone knew it. Something was going to happen: something powerful, miraculous, antici- pated, yet always unexpected. This was not the first time this evangelist had visited.

The altar call was no surprise. It followed the purest Southern Pentecostal tradition: first those who needed salvation, then a plea for those who had never received the baptism, then, "Do you need healing in your body? Tonight is your night!" Then it happened, completely random, unex- plained, seemingly without any justification: individuals began to be called out. Grown men trembled inwardly; little boys shook with fear. "You, right there, yes, I mean you! Come up here! God has got something for you tonight!" One by one they came, some hesitantly, some eagerly, some stiff and reserved, some broken and weeping.

The last to be called was a twelve-year-old boy. He came with his heart in his throat, sure that some secret sin of his was about to be aired before the whole church. Instead, a warm arm was placed around him. A soft voice said, "Tonight you are going to help me pray for these people." What surprise, what relief, what confusion: God wanted him to pray for these people?

Halfway down the men's side of the altar, this wisp of a woman stood before a virtual Goliath—well over six feet tall, easily surpassing 250, arms crossed above his ample belly, his face a poster for unbelief and skepticism. The young boy recognized him as the unsaved husband of a new convert.

That singular sharp eye bored into that unbelieving face. A pointed finger jabbed at least three inches into that ample belly. The voice thundered with certainty and confidence: "Today you were diagnosed with cancer. It's right here."

The finger jabbed again. "You haven't told your wife or your children, but tonight God is going to heal you." The unbelief and skepticism were instantly replaced with astonishment; eyes that had glared moments before were now open wide with shock and surprise and began to tear. The only words that could escape his slacked mouth were ones of amazement: "But I never told anyone!"

That night, God healed and saved that unbelieving husband. That night, God taught me a lesson about faith and healing. You see, I was that twelve-year-old boy. That intimidating evangelist? She was my grandmother.

At ninety-three, she was privileged to go on to her reward, being reunited with her husband, her family, her grandchildren that had gone before her. Oh, but most of all, with her precious Savior, whom she served so faithfully so many years. Others may question the miraculous use of the gifts of the Holy Spirit today; I was blessed to watch them in action as a twelve-year-old boy.

He Shall Give His Angels Charge over You

I stare down at the fire-blackened gas hose and whispered a prayer of thanks. The smell of burnt rubber lingers in the air. The hose is burnt, the exterior bubbled and crisp like food spilled on the bottom of an oven. The wall is scorched by the flames. The back of our gas dryer is blackened by soot. I listen to Renee describe how helpless she felt when she discovered that the water was off when the fire started. Thankfully, no one was injured, and no permanent damage was done. This was our second brush with danger today.

Living in a developing country makes you a little more leery of accidents. Here there is no 911. The police often don't answer the phone, or if they do pick up, they often insist that they don't have enough gas in the truck to respond to calls for help.

The Forestry Department's office is located three hundred yards from the one and only fire station. A fire started one night a few years back, and it took the fire department forty-five minutes to respond. The office burned to the ground.

A trip to the emergency room when our oldest son, Bryan, had appendicitis yielded an overnight stay where we saw not one medical doctor and were informed that the island's only surgeon would be leaving early the next morning before he could perform the surgery. I called him at home and asked him what I was supposed to do about my son. "Give him antibiotics," he said. "They will probably hold him till I get back." He was going away for a week!

The moral of the story is that you don't want to have an accident, emergency, or illness while in Vanuatu. The standing joke in the expatriate community is "Feel a pain? Catch a plane!" The truth of the matter is that no matter how much you try to prevent them, accidents are a part of life, and when far from home, you lean more heavily on God.

I will never forget the day that Bryan, age three, entered the house crying and saying that he had fallen. We looked him over for cuts and bruises and, finding none, concluded that it had been only a minor tumble. When he continued to cry, we asked him to show us where he had fallen. We were stunned when he pointed to the rail of our second-story balcony. He had been trying to copy a neighbor kid who did a balancing act on the top of the rail. We could only assume that an angel broke his fall that day.

Earlier in the day, Nathan, our missionary associate who is overseeing the construction and startup of Jubilee Christian School, had his own brush with danger. After trimming out his bathroom window, he stepped back to examine his handiwork. Unfortunately, he momentarily forgot the open septic tank behind him. The septic tank, which is still under construction, is seven feet deep, has a concrete floor, and, most ominously, has three-foot-long lengths of rebar sticking up from the floor as starter bars for cement block. The potential for grave bodily harm in the form of broken bones—or worse, being impaled by the rebar—was great. Thankfully, Nathan walked away with only bruises and a sore back.

George, a first-generation Christian from the Tiali tribe in Big Bay, was working with Nathan when he fell. He and his son provided the bamboo and are weaving it into siding for Nathan and Jennifer's house. He told me later, "Missionary, if we were just doing normal work, he would have been hurt badly. It is because we are doing God's work that he is unharmed." I think he is right.

When I returned home with a hobbling Nathan, I was greeted at the door by Renee. "We had a little excitement today," she told me. My eyes lit up. We have been praying for funds for construction on the new campus. Had a major donor called up to say they would be helping us? Noting the expression on my face, Renee set me straight: "Not that kind of excitement."

That's when she led me to our fire-blackened laundry room. Normally this room would have towels and soiled clothes waiting to be washed. The gas lines to both the dryer and the hot-water heater run through it. The potential for a conflagration was great. Thankfully, the laundry room was completely empty today. Thankfully, a door suddenly slamming drew my son's attention. Thankfully, he had the presence of mind to rush to the propane tank and turn off the flow of gas.

Psalms 91:11 is one of many verses that we have claimed as missionaries: "For he shall give his angels charge over thee, to keep thee in all thy ways." (KJV)

Yes, we have times of trial and even pain. Being a missionary doesn't exempt one from hardship. However, being far from home removes you from the normal support structures that provide far more security than we often realize. Living on an island where help doesn't come in the form of uniformed police officers, heavy-coated firefighters, or white-coated doctors makes you even more dependent on God—and all the more thankful that he shall give his angels charge over thee!

An Unexpected Invitation

Chief Wabak, from the village of Lonlipli, pulled me aside the last day of the Health Care Ministries Clinic in his area. "Missionary, we want to do something special for you and the team," he said. "Maybe we could do a traditional dance. We would let you take pictures." Vivid images of naked villagers that the team had treated paraded through my mind. I was quite sure that watching them dance in little more than their birthday suits was not something the team would be interested in.

When you go into pre-Christian areas, it is understood that you will have to adapt to their ways, not the other way around. Part of that adaptation in Vanuatu is dealing with what most Americans would consider to be immodest styles of dress, or rather the lack thereof.

On the island of Pentecost, where we were conducting the clinic, the style of dress is decidedly different than Santo. Here the men wear a *nambas*, a penis wrapper; this wrap is secured around the waist by a vine, and everything else is fully revealed. The women on Pentecost wear heavy grass skirts that actually provide a modest covering from the waist down.

Getting used to this can be a bit disconcerting at first. Alecia, our seventeen-year-old daughter, was conducting the registration for the clinic. The patients would sit next to her on a bamboo bench while giving details like name, age, and home village. As long as the patients were women or teenage girls, this was just fine. The first time a man sat beside her in only a nambas, she turned beet red.

Clearly, a traditional dance was not an option. What could the chief give in return as an expression of thanks?

"Chief," I said, "I think if you really want to show your appreciation to the team, the best way you could do that would be to let us share the gospel with your people." There was a conspicuous silence in the conversation. I could see that the chief was struggling with this idea. Before we came to this part of Pentecost, we had been warned by pastors of neighboring villages that we would not be allowed to enter Lonlipli as missionaries, much less share the gospel. It is a point of pride among custom chiefs to keep their village "pure" and free from Christian influence. However, in the months preceding this clinic, people from all over America had been praying that villages like his would be opened to the gospel. This was the moment of truth.

After a pregnant pause in the conversation, the chief spoke. "Missionary, I think that I would like to express my appreciation to the team for bringing medical care to my people. Would you be willing to come to Lonlipli and share with my people?"

Sunday morning we set out early from our camp on the coast at Ranputor. A truck carried us as far as Ponmil, the site of the week's clinic. There, high on the mountainous spine of Pentecost, clouds wrapped the tops of the mountains in wispy cloaks. Trees faded in and out of view as the clouds swept through the narrow pass at Ponmil. The muddy path plunged off the side of the mountain through a grove of giant tree ferns.

We made our way down the side of the mountain, through a pristine alpine valley with a spring at its head, and over a small hill before the village came into sight. Chief Wabak greeted us with his family and began proudly showing off his village. At the *nasara*, or dancing ground, we were met by stern-looking village elders.

A rapid-fire exchange took place in the Sa language. The chief then beckoned me aside. It was clear that his invitation to us had not met with approval from the other men in the village. After a few minutes' negotiation, it was agreed that the others would look around the village while I visited with the chief and his elders in the *nakamal*, or men's house. Nervous tension filled the air; the chief was embarrassed by his elders' reaction yet afraid to allow me to share the gospel. I prayed that God would give me wisdom and open their hearts.

Squatting beside a hearth of "holy fire," I began to ask them questions about their customs and share the customs of various tribes that I had learned about in my travels around Vanuatu. We swapped stories for the better part of an hour. Gradually the tension began to melt away. "Chief, I have come here today as a friend. I want today to be the beginning of a friendship between you and me. What I want to share with you this morning I want to share because I am your friend."

"Missionary, let's go to my house; there the women and children can join us," he replied.

There, in a simple hut, surrounded by skeptical elders, inquisitive women, and children, I shared the good news that moves men from life to death.

Pastor Joe

"Missionary, we are super impressed with Pastor Joe.[1] We feel like God wants us to support his ministry on a monthly basis. Can you tell us the best way to do so?"

I groan in spite of myself. Over and over this scenario has played out. I know it is the best of intentions that prompts the question. The kind-hearted lady speaking with me is on her first mission trip. Both her pastor and I had advised her group to avoid making promises to anyone while they were here. This is boilerplate orientation for all short-term teams coming to Vanuatu.

I don't want to ask because I already know the answer. "Did you mention this to him?"

"Yes," she replies, her face clouding with worry. "Should I not have? We really do want to help him." I try not to, really I do, but I groan again. I know Pastor Joe is impressive. He has a beautiful young wife and three adorable children that are always immaculately groomed, and he speaks fantastic English.

There are so many layers of why this is a bad idea.

There is a biblical pattern for the support of the ministry. In the Old Testament, the priests and the Levites were supported by the tithes and offerings presented at the temple. As they served the Lord and the people, their needs were met. Whenever temple worship declined, they felt the

---

1 Not his real name.

pinch of decreased revenue, promoting them to greater diligence in teaching God's law.

In the New Testament, believers participated in both proportional giving (tithes) and freewill offerings. Paul taught that teachers and church leaders should be provided for by those they ministered to, asking "Who tends a flock without getting some milk?" (1 Cor. 9:7 [ESV]). He bases his arguments on the law command, "You shall not muzzle an ox when it treads out the grain" (1 Cor. 9:9 [ESV]). Finally, in verse 11, he asks, "If we have sown spiritual things among you, is it too much if we reap material things from you?"

The principle is straightforward: those who have a spiritual ministry should be supported materially by those they serve. Paul reaffirms it in his letter to Timothy. He tells Timothy, "Let the elders who rule well be considered worthy of double honor, especially those who labor in preaching and teaching. For the scripture says, 'You shall not muzzle an ox when it treads out the grain,' and, 'The laborer deserves his wages'" (1 Tim. 7:17–18 [ESV]).

The picture of the ox is a graphic illustration. Its feet and weight are responsible for the grain breaking free of the chaff. As it works, in the very process of freeing the grain, it bows its head and partakes of the grain. The workers receive their wages directly from the point of ministry.

The sole exception to this principal is found in 3 John: "For they have gone out for the sake of the name, accepting nothing from the Gentiles. Therefore we ought to support people like these, that we may be fellow workers for the truth" (3 John 1:7–8 [ESV]). Those who are planting a church among the unreached should be supported either by their own labor, commonly known as tent making, or by an existing church.

"Ah, missionary, you belabor the point," you say. "You just want all the support to come to you. You want to control the funds!" At first, such accusations hurt. I questioned myself and my motives: Was it possible? Now, I am immune. I have heard these accusations till I am jaded toward them.

It's true that missionaries are sometimes manipulative and controlling. It's true that money is sometimes misused in missions to empower missionaries. I confess, early in my career, I made the mistake of attempting to purchase influence. It was wrong.

Let me tell you some other things that are also true. Every time we ignore the principles of God's word and create a work-around, it is to our detriment, every time. It doesn't matter if we are discussing the principles of how we handle our money, our marriage, our children, or our neighbors. If we disregard the principles of his word, it causes grief. Guess what? That's true in missions as well.

Renee and I have been on the ground in missions for sixteen years as I write. I'm not speculating with you about possible effects; here is what I have observed about local pastors being supported by overseas funds.

1. **It weakens the pastor's influence in the community.** The pastor is seen as a puppet of foreign organizations, unable to support himself and unable to make decisions.
2. **It weakens the pastor's initiative for ministry.** The pastor no longer feels the economic crunch of a struggling work. One of the motivators built into the biblical plan of ministry is lost.
3. **It weakens the pastor's faith in God.** Ministry becomes limited to what his foreign donor is willing to pay for, not wherever God is leading him.
4. **It weakens the average church member's financial situation.** Since the pastor is being supported by foreign funds, average church members feel free to withhold their tithes and reduce their gifts. Giving in the local church declines. The blessings believers experience when they give disappear.
5. **It weakens the pastor's character.** As his focus changes from God to money, his entire character suffers.
6. **It weakens the pastor's relationship with fellow pastors.** Greed and jealousy are universal human failings. Once a pastor becomes supported by foreign funds, his only friends are those who hope to use him to gain money or access to overseas donors.
7. **It becomes a pattern of behavior.** Many pastors supported by foreign funds begin milking multiple sources. They become little more than religious con men.

But you say, "The pastor we support is different!" How would you know? Do you really believe that what you see during your short visit to his field represents everyday reality?

Maybe you are right. Maybe the local pastor you support is different. Yet for every one of those exceptional pastors, I, as a missionary, get to watch a dozen ministers with great potential be destroyed by your best intentions.

Pastor Joe? He is one of the success stories.

This sweet lady was the third full-time sponsor for him and his family. She even sponsored him and his wife to visit her. While there, he used her computer to search the web for porn, which led to an investigation by her church, revealing not only his porn addiction but the fact that he had been lying to his supporting churches regarding the amount of funds he was receiving and the ministry in which he was engaged.

The resulting discipline saved his soul, his family, and his ministry. Today Pastor Joe is a very successful pastor in Vanuatu doing an amazing work for God, and he is supported by those to whom he ministers.

The Matter of a Key

It was a sultry, hot Friday, the kind of day when you can stand in the shade with a fan and still soak your shirt with sweat. The two miles of open water between Aore and Luganville were lying flat, unruffled by as much as a puff of breeze. A hot, tropical sun beat down relentlessly on the brilliant blue water, the white coral beaches, and a very dusty little town. As I pulled my truck into the unpaved parking lot of our local hardware store, the dust stirred up by the truck hung stationary in the air above. Undisturbed by wind, it stalled momentarily in the heavy, humid air before settling down to coat the truck, sidewalk, and flower beds in yet another coat of white dust. On days like this, even the flies move slow.

Inside the hardware store, it was cleaner but still brutally hot. High above, giant ceiling fans turned in slow motion as if they too were filled with lethargy, each rotation exchanging sticky, hot air below with more of the same from above. Discount bins littered the front of the store, filled with odds and ends that the management was trying valiantly to move, from hand tools to superglue. Yellow sale notices announcing unbelievably low prices hung limply on the sides of the bins, refusing to even flutter in the wake of the ceiling fans.

I was greeted by the manager and his staff. I had their undivided attention; no one else was crazy enough to be stirring around in this heat. I held up my truck key. "Can you cut me a copy of this?" I asked. Truck keys have been a bit of a saga for us. When we purchased the truck, we were supplied with only one key; we were told we would receive the second by post soon. I was a new missionary, so my gullibility is forgivable. The key never came. It took six years to finally convince the dealership that I needed a second key.

Once we had a second key, we quickly disposed of it. Truck keys just have a way of disappearing, especially around water. The first key disappeared temporarily during a swimming trip at the White Grass waterfall. Renee, the nonswimmer that day, was holding the key when she slipped on a mossy rock. Renee went down; the key went up and then down, down, down. After an extended search using snorkeling gear, the key was rescued. The second story of the key entails a little boy's bad habits and dirty diapers that were not checked well enough before being flushed away. We know where that key is but are just not motivated enough to go after it. Over time we adjusted to having only one key again—that is, until our local hardware store installed a key-cutting machine and declared it open for cutting.

The manager found it incredulous that I would even ask such a question. "Can we cut a copy of your key? Of course we can!" He then proceeded to brag about the young man who had been trained to cut keys. "If he cuts it, you don't even have to test it; he is the best in town." Of course, when you are the only key cutter in town, it is not too hard to be the best. I suppose we could just as honestly say that he is without a doubt the worst key cutter in town as well, but it sounds better to say he is the best, so the best it is. I don't know if the manager really had that much confidence in the young man or if he was just bored by the total lack of customers and desperate to make conversation.

While the clerk disappeared into another section of the store, the manager began trying to convince me to purchase the hand tools in his discount bin. "Look at this!" he exclaimed. "A hacksaw for just three ninety-nine. Have you ever purchased a hacksaw for less?" he asked. When I mentioned that I had purchased a half dozen of those same hacksaws from the previous manager at just thirty-nine cents each, his face fell. "I heard about that," he lamented. Eventually I picked up a few tools just to make the poor fellow feel better, and then we chewed the fat while waiting for the key-cutting clerk to return.

The key fit, so I paid for it. I took it home and gave it to our new missionary associates. "Now you have your own key," I told them. No more trading the one key back and forth; it was a great day. They greeted the news with smiles. On Saturday morning, they made a trip to town, using their new key for the first time. A few hours later, they returned. "I'm afraid there is something wrong with the truck," one told me. The pungent aroma of burning insulation greeted me outside. "While we were driving home, the electrical things started to fail."

I found the new key firmly lodged in the ignition and with no intention of coming out. Try as I might, I could not make the key budge. It had entered the ignition easy enough and even started the truck; however, it seemed the new key, cut by the best key cutter in town, had stuck in the start position, burning out the starter before overloading the entire electrical system.

Poppy, the local mechanic, greeted me with a wide smile. Why not? I have been keeping him and his family well fed. "Pastor," he said with a heavy Australian twang, "what in the bloody 'ell is wrong with your truck this time?" In his midfifties, five foot eight, and a good 300lbs, Poppy was wearing only a small black pair of swim trunks. His bald head was offset by a very hairy rest of him, and his chest and legs bore thick white scars from open heart surgery. His wide grin revealed badly rotting teeth.

I smiled before answering. "Well, you see, Poppy, it is a matter of a key."

Why Does the Way of the Wicked Prosper?

You are always righteous, O LORD, when I bring a case before you. Yet I would speak with you about your justice: Why does the way of the wicked prosper? Why do all the faithless live at ease? —Jeremiah 12:1 (NIV)

I wonder who got to Jeremiah. Was it a new house for his brother-in-law? Maybe the first in his neighborhood to pick up the new iPhone was a scoundrel who had borrowed Jeremiah's tools and never returned them. Or was it just their relatively easy lifestyle in light of his hardships? All I know is that I can identify with the prophet.

Dusk is falling at Sanma Bible Training Center. The sun has slid behind the mountains to the west, becoming a crimson memory. Its last rays gild the clouds and paint the darkening sky a kaleidoscope of color ranging from indigo in the east to salmon in the west. The coral road and the exposed white pine frame of the house I am working on seem to glow in the gathering darkness.

I am standing on scaffolding high above the campus giving me my first bird's-eye view. We have just finished hanging half of the rafters of a staff house. Tomorrow we will finish the task. The five acres that we have cleared for the first phase of the campus is spread out before me in a trapezoid, like an enormous triangle that has had the top chopped off by the road.

I am amazed at the transformation. A few short months ago, it was impenetrable jungle; today it is cleared, with clearly defined building sites and neat rows of gardens filling the open spaces. Cleaning those five acres required thousands of hot, sweaty man-hours with a hook and machete. I shudder when I think of the next twenty-two acres.

In my mind's eye, I see the remainder of the buildings that will make up this phase of the campus. The chapel centered on the bottom of the trapezoid is the defining building; everything else is placed in relation to it. Its high vaulted roof, short walls, and richly colored teak posts give it an open and airy feel. The *natanggura* thatch shines coppery as the wind dances with the leaves hanging from the edge of the thatch.

On the far fence line is the classroom and kitchen for Jubilee Christian School. There, under the shade of seventy-foot-high whitewoods, I see pint-sized desks and miniature chairs, dusty chalkboards, bulletin boards with ABCs and 123s, a globe, and a playground full of brightly colored equipment.

Here on this fence line, on either side of the house I am currently building, I see cottages with woven bamboo walls facing the park-like green in the center. The warm light of kerosene lanterns glows through their windows and spills out of cracks in the walls.

Scattered drops of rain bring me back to the present, and I cringe inwardly when I look at the white pine glowing in the twilight. Where will I get the funds to pay for the roof to cover it? I worry about the effect of torrential rains and blazing days of sun on the exposed timber. "Lord," I pray, "I need help." If I don't have the funds to finish this house, how will I ever complete the other buildings? Maybe it is different for other missionaries. Maybe I overreach. But the reality is that we are always engaged in projects that require twice as much funding as my monthly budget provides.

Being a missionary has changed my perspective of faith. I used to wrestle with the words of Hebrews: "Faith is the substance of things hoped for, the evidence of things not seen." I strained to produce a feeling of great faith, anticipating I would be given great miracles. In reality, Hebrews 11 is filled with stories not of what great men and women *received* by faith but what they *did* by faith.

Faith, as I understand it now, involves utter certainty in what God is leading you to do so that you can visualize what will be, "the evidence of things not seen," that which from the perspective of eternity is, yet presently in time is not. By faith you can reach into eternity and feel the very "substance of things hoped for," grasp that which God has promised, and forcibly wrest it into time. No, this is not some type of spiritual conjuring act; it involves mud on the boots, hands on the tools, and a lot of sweat and sore muscles.

Building by faith sometimes requires a whole different approach. Brush that could be cleared in an hour by a tractor instead is cleared by a team of volunteers sweating away a Saturday. Posts that could be lifted into place by a crane in a few moments are pulled into place by teams of straining men and a block and tackle. Major cement pours are scheduled not around the weather but around the availability of large groups of volunteers.

On my way home, I pass a number of buildings under construction: a new bank, another story added to a large office building, a new store—all commercial buildings dedicated simply to making money. Some of them are owned by businessmen whose practices border on predatory. Soon they will be accumulating even more wealth out of the poverty of Vanuatu.

I see daily progress; teams of workers swarm over the sites like ants on an anthill, and heavy equipment abounds, accomplishing in an hour tasks that take us days. Hard hat–clad contractors gesture, and legions of workers scramble to do their bidding. I groan when I see their massive progress compared to the snail's pace we are working at.

I find myself echoing the words of Jeremiah: "You are always righteous, O LORD.... Yet...why does the way of the wicked prosper? Why do all the faithless live at ease?" (NIV)

Flashlight Medicine

My sleep was interrupted by the throbbing rumble of diesel engines. I could hear the sound of metal clanking over the surf and the voices of men shouting. The ship was here! I dressed quickly and made my way out of the two-room house we were staying in, careful to not step on kids as I felt my way through the dark. Grabbing a small flashlight hanging from the nail by the door, I made my way out into the rainy night. There, wallowing in the surf, was the barge *Tina 1*. I made my way down the pebble beach to the streams of men coming and going from the ship. Kava, peanuts, and taro were being loaded on board for shipment to Port Vila. Soap, fuel, rice, and kerosene were being off-loaded. There was no wharf; the *Tina 1* simply pushed as far as possible against the beach, and men carried the supplies through the breaking waves.

I saw Pastor Falau among the baggage. There, in a tangled heap, were the foot lockers I had packed weeks ago on Santo. Food, mosquito nets, medical equipment, shower tents, toilet seats, gospel literature, lights, a generator, desks—everything needed by a team of doctors and dentists for a week-long medical outreach, except.... "Falau, where are our chairs?" Seventeen bright-pink plastic chairs with my name and phone number all over them—they should have been there on the beach. Clearly they were not. "I don't know, missionary. I think they lost them." I made my way through the surf to find the supercargo of the ship. He was busy supervising the loading of cargo from Pentecost. I introduced myself and asked about my chairs, "Sorry, missionary, another white man took them off the ship a few villages back."

Logistics can be a nightmare in Vanuatu. Ships arrive late or sometimes never at all. One ship pulled into the wharf on Tanna with the materials to build two churches. The captain announced to the pastor who had been waiting for them that he had "lost" two tons of cement. How do you lose two tons of anything? We waited nearly a year for him to "find" them. Thankfully, the pastor's cousin is the harbor master. It took the threat of his ship losing the privilege of using the wharf to jog the captain's memory as to where he had misplaced them.

In Vanuatu you get used to such delays. You can rage against the system, but all that gets you is enemies, ensuring that your cargo never arrives. The tension for a missionary comes when you have a team of visiting Americans. Americans have the unrealistic expectation that when they pay for a service, it should be delivered, a concept totally foreign to this part of the world. To try to avoid frustration, you make your plans well in advance. Since I knew I had a team of doctors coming to Pentecost and they would need supplies for a successful clinic, I shipped our cargo weeks before they arrived in the country.

My first sign that something was wrong was a 2:00 a.m. phone call from Pastor Falau, our point man for this outreach. "Missionary, you better call the ship; they are passing by us without stopping."

I searched through my contacts and found a number for the captain. I introduced myself and explained my concern: "I have a shipment of medical supplies for Ranputor. My men there tell me you aren't stopping."

"That's right," he replied. "The ship is full." A fifteen-minute conversation yielded no change. The fact that I had paid for my cargo to be delivered to Ranputor was insignificant. He had enough cargo to go to Port Vila, so he was headed to the big city. "Don't worry," he told me. "It will be there next week. I will make it my first stop when I head north."

Weeks later I greeted our team from Health Care Ministries, welcoming them to Vanuatu, giving a brief introduction to the culture, and advising them of the schedule for the week. "There is one small hitch though; our supplies have still not been delivered to our base camp. The shipping company emphatically assured me that they will be there before we arrive tomorrow. However, we should be prepared to rough it if need be." Nods greeted my announcement, and attention was turned to more pressing matters, like changing money and finding bottled water. If the shipping company promised it would be there, then there shouldn't be a problem, right? I was the only one present who understood how much that promise was worth.

Two days later, in Ponmil, we began setting up for our first day of clinic. "Bryan, do we have a pressure cooker to sterilize instruments? Lights for the exam rooms? A generator? Any food we recognize? A water purifier for drinking water? Mosquito repellent? Tables for the exam rooms? Chairs for our patients?" After a few minutes, the team started answering their own questions: "Yes, on the ship."

A lesser team of medical professionals would have thrown up their hands in exasperation and said, "It can't be done." But this team found a way to minister to the sick and wounded of Pentecost in spite of what was missing. They created chemical baths to sterilize instruments, ate food with names they could not pronounce, suffered through the mosquitoes, prayed over questionable water, and hung flashlights from the rafters so that they could see patients. Two days into their trip, the ship finally arrived, minus the chairs.

No, it was not what we wanted or what we had planned. But the people of Ponmil got the chance to see the love of Christ displayed through flashlight medicine. Two hundred and fifty people found Christ as their Savior as a result of the team's efforts.

Missionary Kids

It felt good to be home.

The building was air-conditioned, with padded pews. The worship service featured familiar songs I had grown up with. The service was orderly, with any potentially disruptive children off in age-appropriate ministries. The sermon was in my own language, and the order of service was one that felt familiar and welcome. We were in our home church for the first time after a four-year term of service in Vanuatu. Did I miss Vanuatu? Sure, but it felt so spiritually refreshing to be home. I was sure my whole family felt the same way.

At the end of the service, the altars were opened for prayer. How I had missed these times of cooperate prayer. The cultural shyness of Ni-Vanuatu makes cooperate prayer around altars a rare event in Vanuatu. They prefer a prayer closet to a public altar. While intellectually I could understand, spiritually and emotionally I longed for an extended period of prayer at the altar.

In our home church, the men typically pray on the right side of the building and the women on the left. I couldn't begin to explain why the altar time is segregated or why the men have the right versus the left. Everyone just knows that is the way things are. Renee and I followed our children down the aisle that evening. Our son moved to the right altar either instinctively, following the flow of other men and boys, or just got lucky. Our daughter followed her brother. It's crazy, but you could immediately read on the faces of several men around her that this was awkward. Didn't she know which side of the church she was supposed to go to for prayer?

Renee and I formed a protective cocoon around her that evening to keep her from discovering the feelings of others and to try to keep others from feeling awkward. After all, who could be offended by a family praying together? Maybe you are judging my home church. "How could anyone be so silly as to have segregated altars?" you might ask. Yet for us, it exposed a much deeper issue: the things that everyone knows but our children don't.

Welcome to the world of MKs, or missionary kids. Call me naïve, but when we first prepared to become missionaries, I didn't think much about the impact it would have on our children. Watching my daughter tear up as we sold her toys in preparation for leaving for the field for the first time felt like a dagger in my gut. It was then I realized how life altering this would be for them. They would not grow up American; they would have only occasional, fleeting memories of grandparents; they wouldn't know their cousins, shoot off fireworks on the Fourth of July, know to wear green on Saint Patrick's Day, learn to have turkey for Thanksgiving or the crush of family gathered at Christmas. What was normal for me would be foreign to them.

There are millions of facets of life that are never discussed because everyone knows them, unspoken rules of behavior that we seldom have thought through and would be at a complete loss to explain. Everybody knows that is the way things are done, right? People who miss these cues are considered socially awkward. People who refuse to comply are considered to be nonconformist or just slightly off. If a person is obviously foreign, then we make allowances for them. We assume that they are still learning and pretend that yes, the way they are doing things is right, to a point. However, if a person looks the same as us, there is an expectation that they should know and follow the rules. The MK looks the same but doesn't know the rules.

Consider for a moment nonverbals. Communication theorists tell us that more than 75 percent of all communication is unspoken. This includes everything from space, how close you stand to others, posture, hand expressions, tone of voice, pitch, clothing styles, hairstyle, eye contact to facial expressions.

Posture indicates attention or disrespect, interest or boredom. On Malakula, an island in Vanuatu, women are forbidden to rise above the level of a man's head. Women who want to exit a church where men are seated must stoop in an exaggerated show of respect as they pass the men to avoid breaking this taboo. Imagine our chagrin when our daughter followed this custom in exiting a church service in America. In her mind, she was showing respect. To most of the church members, her behavior was odd, irrational, and distracting. Why didn't she act normal?

A nod means yes, right? Only in Vanuatu you don't express yes with a nod but with a subtle movement of the eyebrows. After growing up in Vanuatu, it is only natural that our children would use this gesture to answer in the affirmative. The problem? The same subtle movement is interpreted in America as being forward and flirtatious.

I could continue with hundreds of examples. It's hard for someone who has lived exclusively in their own culture to realize just how all-pervasive culture is. Unintentionally MKs misinterpret, and are misinterpreted by, nearly everyone around them hundreds of times a day. Often they are confused, feel misunderstood and judged. Tragically, because they don't fit in, they often choose for friends, or are chosen as friends by, others who are nonconformists and loners. The very people they don't need to be learning social cues from become their mentors.

What can be done? Parents can prepare themselves for the impact their missions service will have on their children, and develop a strategy to help their kids through the difficult times. Educate yourself. You aren't the first missionary; there is a wealth of books and materials that will be helpful.

Do what you can to minimize the turmoil. Studies have shown that it is not the intensity of transition but the frequency of transitions that causes adjustment issues for MKs. The trend in missions is toward shorter terms of ministry of six months to two years. Ironically, this is the opposite of what children need most, stability and constancy.

Make your home a bastion of American culture. Attempts to fully integrate themselves in a second culture by missionaries are rarely successful. When missionaries adopt local housing, clothing, food, hygiene levels, and language within the home, internal stress normally causes burnout or sickness in just a few years' time. In your home, use English, celebrate American holidays in American ways with fellow Americans if they are near, wear American clothes, and relate to your spouse, children, and Western guests in American ways. Yes, you are here to serve the locals and you want to become all things to all men, but the odds are your children will live out their adult lives in America. Prepare them for that future.

Expose your children to America. We were thankful that by our raising our kids overseas, they would not be exposed to many of the worst aspects of American culture. Particularly, we were thankful there would be no television, and we followed a zero-movie policy in our home.

Then, the first time we returned to America, our children were confused and amazed by an elevator and positively panicked by an escalator. We faced endless questions about why Americans drove on the wrong side of the road and why they stopped at red lights and why they waited at crosswalks. An older missionary, Robert Holmes, spoke very directly to us to let our kids watch American movies so that they would have a glimpse into American popular culture.

What can the sending church do? Anticipate the needs of MKs. Expect them to be a little different. Give them space to grieve. It is okay for them to like some things about their host country better than they like America. It doesn't mean they are unpatriotic. It just means they miss home.

Don't be offended when they question the status quo. You may uncritically assume the way your church does things is the right way. An MK doesn't carry the baggage of your assumptions. They can be far more objective observers.

Each MK needs a mentor when he or she gets home. Often, young people who would make good cultural mentors for MKs already have a full set of friends. They are not looking for new friends. Churches need to be intentional about encouraging at least one well-adjusted, spiritually grounded young person to adopt MKs when they return from the field.

MKs are a special group of kids, obviously very dear to my heart. They are the product of families who have sacrificed all for the kingdom. Whatever you do, don't sacrifice these kids. As a church body, let's embrace them so that they can reach their full potential in Christ.

An Empty Pot

The first light of morning peeks into my bedroom through the thousand pinholes of woven bamboo walls. A playful breeze toys with the thin curtain, fluttering it up into the air, allowing the sunlight to play over my face flirtatiously. I stir, trying to find an angle to hide my face from the light. Little feet scrape on the cement floor; a small voice calls "Mommy" through our fabric door. The breeze and the sun have been playing the same games in Eli's room as well. Now he wants breakfast. Surrendering to the inevitable, I roll off the thin mat serving as our bed and prepare to face the day.

The guest house at Wunpuku sits across the churchyard from the stage and the impromptu kitchen established for our visit. I step out the door onto the black pebble veranda and duck under the low-hanging eave of the *natanggura* roof. Before me, the churchyard stretches out in a long rectangle of a hundred yards of closely cropped grass that forms a thin carpet over black sand. The church, its unpainted, weathered wood walls glowing in the early morning light, defines the right side of the rectangle. The kitchen and crusade stage sit at the far end. On the left, a hedge of hibiscus broken by mango trees marks the final boundary of the yard.

I stand blinking in the early morning sun, soaking up its rays, stretching and slowly waking up. Something is missing. My eyes slide over the church again, the stage, the kitchen, the towering mango trees, the thin veil of grass, the large round black stones that dot the churchyard. Everything is here, and yet something is not. Renee joins me, and we begin our trek across the yard, toward coffee. The absence nags at the back of my mind, but short of my morning caffeine, I struggle to put my finger on it.

The kitchen is a tiny shack. It has a low, sloping thatch roof. The back wall of rough weathered planks hosts the only door. Each end sports a half wall to facilitate the breeze; the front wall ends at elbow height in a bar comprised of a thick slab of hardwood ripped from a log with a chainsaw. The inside of the kitchen features two low shelves for food prep and dish washing and a dirt floor. A steaming kettle and coffee cups rest on the bar. I quietly greet the mama behind the bar, give my instant coffee package a good shake, stir the contents into the waiting cup, and take a sip. Slowly the world begins to come into focus.

Half a cup later and I am ready for some muted conversation. I notice Pastor Kaulfao sitting on the crusade stage and slowly make my way over to him. My "morning, Pastor" is greeted with a look of exasperation. I look back at the mama behind the bar at the kitchen. I notice that her face too has a strained look. That obscure absence tugs at my mind again. What am I missing here?

Yesterday had been a day of preparation and anticipation. Midmorning the young men from the village, accompanied by a yelping pack of dogs, had headed to a nearby plantation to kill a steer. Killing cattle in Vanuatu is no small matter. A prime steer sells for $400, twice the average monthly wage in Vanuatu. Cattle are not killed every day. But tomorrow was not just any day; tomorrow was Independence Day. Midafternoon the triumphant crew returned with beef quarters swinging from poles suspended across shoulders, dripping palm frond baskets of organs and the youngest member toting the severed head by one of the horns.

The men assembled at a seaside bamboo table and began the task of butchering. The women built an enormous bonfire and then proceeded to heap hundreds of round black stones on top of the flaming wood. The young men and boys squatted around a cooking fire, roasting bits of heart and liver over an open flame. The dogs milled just out of reach of threatening feet and sticks, hoping for scraps and snapping and quarreling over any fragments tossed their way.

The men finished the butchering and lay back on the table to watch the sun prepare to bathe in the ocean. The young men polished off the portions they were given. The women's fire burned down until there were only a few burning bits of log, glowing charcoal, and hundreds of rocks, translucent red with heat.

With enormous tongs of bamboo, the women pulled the last burning pieces of wood and charcoal from the heap and arranged the glowing stones in a tight circle. Carefully they layered the stones with leaves and then arranged the meat over the leaves. Finally the head of the steer was stuffed with hot stones and laid beside the rest of the meat. Women and men worked together to seal in the heat of the stones by layering leaves and, finally, heavy burlap bags over the meat. Stones were placed strategically to stop any steam vents.

That evening the dogs warily circled the cooking meat, drawn by the enticing smell but repelled by the heat and swiftly slung stones when they approached too closely. In the service, Pastor Kaulfao proudly announced to the entire village that tomorrow would be a free feast. "All are welcome! We killed a steer today; there will be plenty of meat for everyone. Make sure you bring your whole family!"

In the early hours of the morning, as most of the men were sleeping, the mamas pulled away the steaming layers of leaves, revealing perfectly roasted beef falling off the bones. A few choice pieces were consumed on the spot and the rest piled into an enormous pot. The pot was placed in the church and the doors closed. Then the village slept—everyone but the dogs.

Pastor Kaulfao repeatedly starts to speak but fails to find the words. His mouth opens, then closes, then opens again. Finally he finds the words, strained halting words: "Missionary, the dogs, they got in the church last night."

Suddenly I realize what is missing. The dogs! A normal village in Vanuatu is filled with yapping, fighting, playing, noisy dogs: fat rolling puppies, mangy old sacks of bones, nursing mothers, strutting males. As a rule, dogs in Vanuatu scrounge for their food and find the pickings mighty poor. Most are little more than skin and bones. I look around for the dogs. They are sprawled beneath trees, bellies distended, dreaming contentedly. And in the church sits an empty pot.

What Do You Smell Like?

Everything in Vanuatu is late. Christmas cards arrive in February, birthday packages two weeks to a month after the fact. Church starts at least a half hour after the announced time, and classes resume two weeks after the calendar start to the school year. Holidays come late too. Mother's Day is the second Sunday in May—unless things are not ready yet, in which case it falls on just about any Sunday that is free. So, today is Mother's Day, this year just one week late.

I am not sure what causes it, this perpetual tardiness. Maybe it's the numbing heat and suffocating humidity that makes you feel that you are forcing your way through molasses when you walk. Perhaps it is the product of a culture that never invented time or a calendar. Possibly it comes from being trapped on an island. After all, there is no rush; even if we have to put it off till next week, no one is going anywhere. Church on this rescheduled Mother's Day is scheduled to start at ten; we arrive right on time at half past.

The church is smothered in decorations. Each window is lined with fresh garlands and flowers. The pulpit is hidden behind enormous bouquets. Potted palms adorn the aisles. Fishing line has been strung in a zigzag pattern overhead and covered with clusters of flowers, creating a multicolored

ceiling of blossoms. Pink and white balloons are everywhere. Glittery ban-
ners proclaiming "Merry Christmas" and "Happy New Year" line the walls.
I guess the décor doesn't have to be relevant, just eye-catching.

The ladies' side of the church is awash in pink, like an enormous bottle
of Pepto-Bismol was dumped out and smothered all of the ladies' dresses.
Pink, Pepto-Bismol pink, is the color for Mother's Day in Vanuatu. I have
photos from previous years of huge assemblies of women all dressed in solid
pink dresses. The men's side of the church, by contrast, is nearly empty.
Most of the men are busy preparing the meal to follow. I have to wonder
how many of them are merely using the meal as an excuse to avoid what
experience has taught them can be an incredibly long service.

Even though we are technically a half hour late to service, things are
not ready to start. Most of the women of the church have prepared a special
song, a poem to read, or a testimony to give. We cannot start until they
have all arrived. It is nearly eleven before all the participants in the service
appear and we can begin. The chief's wife signals the other ladies, and a few
of them retreat to the pastor's study for prayer before beginning.

When the service starts, it is obvious that the ladies are well prepared.
Each song is preplanned. Someone has been designated to oversee each part
of the service, from each prayer to taking the offering. Poems are read,
special songs are sung, stories are told, and tears are shed. As each group
of ladies make their way to the front for their performance, the air is filled
with the scent of their perfume. "The nice thing about ladies," I think to
myself, "is that most of the time, they smell nice!" I know that Father's Day
will not be quite so aromatically pleasing.

The first hour passes quickly enough; however, as we move into the
second, things begin to drag. There is a certain weary dread that sets in on
such occasions in Vanuatu. Once we sat through a Mother's Day service that
lasted six hours. Not six hours of refreshing worship or inspiring preaching
but six hours of poetry recitations and rambling monologues. It is hard to
enjoy the service when you are apprehensive about its length.

Amazingly enough, after only an hour and a half, Renee was asked to
the pulpit to share her sermon. She took 2 Timothy 2:20–21 as her text:
"But in a great house there are not only vessels of gold and of silver, but
also of wood and of earth; and some to honor, and some to dishonor. If a
man therefore purge himself from these, he shall be a vessel unto honor,

sanctified, and meet for the master's use, and prepared unto every good work" (KJV).

I watched as she placed two items on the pulpit, a flower vase and a trash can. As she spoke about Christian character in the life of ladies, she nonchalantly began filling the two vessels, the vase with flowers and the trash can with garbage she had brought from home. It was more like a conversation than a sermon, Renee sweetly saying things that might have been offensive to some, except for her sweet demeanor and preoccupation with her flower arrangement.

The initial flowers looked lost in the vase; however, over the course of her sermon, what had been an empty vase filled till beauty and color seemed ready to burst out of it. Occasionally she would pause to savor the scent of the blossoms before continuing. The trash can, on the other hand, was filled with what was obviously foul, smelly refuse.

Bracketed by the vase and the trash can, she read Ephesians 5:2: "Live a life of love, just as Christ loved us and gave himself up for us as a fragrant offering" (NIV), emphasizing the word *fragrant*. Sweetly she asked, "What does your life smell like to God?"

Waiting

Waiting is something that we do a little bit of here in Vanuatu. In fact, I would dare say that I have become a champion waiter, the kind that can endure hours of mindless waiting without losing my cool. Vanuatu changes your perspective about time, patience, and what a reasonable waiting period is.

Nearly everything that you do here requires waiting. To see a teller at the bank is often an hour's wait, then getting approval for your transaction, another wait. If you would like to purchase something from the store—say, butter—then most often you need to wait till the next ship comes in. You arrive on time for church, a wedding, or a funeral? Then you are going to wait, for hours. Need repairs to your truck? 'Fraid you will have to wait for parts to be shipped in from Australia. Need to catch a flight to a neighboring island, and you're checked in on time? Then you are going to wait, and frankly no one can tell you for how long. Numerous times I have waited all day for a plane that never came. Have a medical emergency, need to see a doctor? You can wait, but...

Currently we have an missionary associate couple waiting for a visa. It seems that the immigration department is waiting for the labor department to issue their permit, and the labor department in turn is waiting for the immigration department to issue theirs. This all adds up to a young couple having a very long and frustrating wait, wondering if they are about to be deported. Meanwhile we wait to see who will blink first.

All this waiting has a profound effect on the culture. I would venture a very nonscientific guess that over 50 percent of a Ni-Vanuatu's life is spent waiting. Something has to be done to keep that time from being wasted. In fact, an important pastime has been developed around waiting. It is called *storian*.

Storian reminds me of tales of old men swapping yarns around a cast-iron stove in a country store. Depending on the relationship between the participants, storian can be about anything or nothing. It may involve a couple to a dozen people. It is filled with laughter and tears. Storian is such a pervasive part of life in Vanuatu that the local phone company ran an ad campaign with the slogan "Storian is our life."

Storian is about relationships. If those waiting have an existing relationship, then it revolves around what they have in common, and nothing—trust me, nothing—is sacred. I have witnessed conversations between pastors that would make a locker room full of American high school jocks blush. It is also the primary means of building and repairing relationships in Vanuatu. Want to make a new friend? You must storian.

If there is no known relationship, then the first order of business is to discover one. Two strangers thrown together by the need to wait begin comparing place of birth, family histories in ever-expanding circles till they find a common bond. Even in a country of a quarter million people, if you expand the definition of family broad enough, then nearly everyone is kin. In the absence of a kinship, a mutual friend will suffice. Once a bond has been established, then the storian can begin.

Storian's great benefit is that it turns waiting into a pleasant and useful experience. Some of the most amazing relationships I have had the privilege of having started with a long wait. Missionaries that grasp and master this cultural skill tend to flourish; those who don't tend to remain puzzled outsiders for the duration of their stay.

Pentecost Sunday I was at home taking care of my wife and our sick three-year-old. Drew, our nine-year-old, stayed home as well since he was still running a low-grade fever. So while his mother and little brother slept, Drew and I had a mini-service. As we read the story of Pentecost, the word *wait* stood out to Drew. As a missionary kid, he knows a thing or two about waiting. "So what did they do, Dad? Storian?"

It is a good question: What did they do? A group of disciples of Christ, men and women, apostles and the unnamed. For years they had followed

Christ; the last two months of their lives had been an incredible roller coaster ride. First, one of their own betrayed Christ. Then, in stunned fear, they saw Christ arrested and tried. In despair they watched him die, and in amazement they witnessed his resurrection. They hoped the Risen Lord would usher in his kingdom, and instead he tells them to wait. Wait? What to do while waiting?

As a missionary returning to the States, the great rush is what stands out. Everybody is busy, in a hurry, rushing around; in fact, the only time Americans seem to slow down is called "rush hour." My first month home, I feel like I am standing in the middle of a busy intersection. Everyone is flying by, and I alone am standing still. Thankfully, I have a few good friends who are willing to wait with me and take time to listen to me process the swirl of activity around me.

Thankfully, we don't have to speculate as to how the disciples waited. The scripture record tells us clearly, "They all joined together constantly in prayer." If there is anything painful to Americans, it is waiting. Fast food, express checkout lines, ATMs on every corner—these things symbolize our culture. Give us what we want, and give it to us now! Yet the most valuable opportunities to build relationships, including our relationship with God, are when we wait.

I am sure that over the course of the ten days between Christ's ascension and the outpouring of the Holy Spirit, the disciples slept and ate. We know that they discussed Judas's betrayal and his replacement. But while they waited, they prayed. In fact, they were constantly in prayer. The logical assumption is that if we want to replicate their experience, we need to emulate their actions.

So after we finished discussing the story, Drew and I bowed our heads in prayer, and we waited.

A Piece of Paper

The woman is tall and slender. Her face is pretty. She is waiting to catch the plane. And as is the fashion of departing passengers everywhere, she is making small talk with her friends, eager for the flight to be called and yet dreading saying good-bye. One thing is going through my mind as I watch her. It is a piece of paper she asked me to prepare. It is tucked away in her luggage, small and inconspicuous. Hopefully, it will remain unnoticed, yet the ramifications of its discovery are enormous. A career would be lost. Fines would be imposed. Prison time is very likely. Even death is possible. It is just a piece of paper. Why would someone risk so much for something so insignificant?

In December I was asked to go to what must remain an undisclosed location to speak to people of a nationality that must also be kept quiet. What I can tell you is that they were communist government workers, educated people with degrees and positions, families: people with much to lose. They had asked me to come because they wanted to know, "What is the real meaning of Christmas?"

I spoke that evening on the uniqueness of the birth of Christ. I had been given very careful instructions: do not make an altar call; rather tell them you will be available for further discussions after the message. The reason was ominous: "We know there is a member of the Secret Police present." Considering this warning, I was surprised when this brave woman stood and, with tear-filled eyes, confessed her faith in Christ and her willingness to follow him regardless of the cost. It was an intense moment. I have heard many *say* they would be willing to follow Christ to prison or to death, but I have never heard such a confession under circumstances that would make it likely the price would indeed be paid.

Some weeks later, she followed the Lord in water baptism. Then she sent a message to me: "Would you please prepare for me a baptismal certificate?" A simple piece of paper, one so small, so insignificant, and, honestly, unnecessary. We can be sure Jesus never issued them. Yet this young communist wanted tangible proof of her decision, proof that could oh so easily become evidence. In this day of cavalier Christians, I was awed by the depth of her commitment.

I watch as the flight is called. This brave young woman hugs her friends good-bye, picks up her handbag, tosses a final smile over her shoulder, and walks toward a plane, toward customs agents, toward baggage inspections, toward disgrace and prison time or more if her crime is discovered. I watch with a heart full of respect and a catch in my throat as a song begins to play in my head, "Onward Christian soldier, marching as to war, with the cross of Jesus going on before...."

In Conclusion

"The time of my departure is at hand. I have fought a good fight, I have finished my course, I have kept the faith: Henceforth there is laid up for me a crown of righteousness." —2 Timothy 4:6b–8a (KJV)

How different things look at the end of a matter than at the beginning, or for that matter, even in the midst of a thing. As Paul prepared for the end of his life, he was able to tell Timothy that he had fought well, finished well, and held on to his faith—a significant list of accomplishments. I wonder if in his private musings there weren't some regrets: his rejection of the young John Mark, his irreconcilable conflict with Barnabas, losing Demas. Did Paul ponder the might-have-beens?

In the beginning of missions one is very positive, optimistic, confident. Haven't I been chosen by God? Ordained by my church? Appointed by my mission board? Sponsored by my partners? Trained by my mentors? Surely my mission career will foster significant and meaningful change. My ministry will be valid and valuable. My life will be worth replicating. My home church and supporters believe in me; why shouldn't I? One resolves to be strategic, deliberate, and careful.

The midst of missions is often a blur. Purpose—to represent Christ and have his image formed in our lives—is sometimes trumped by task—to finish this church building, school, or clinic. While the task *should* allow us to more fully recognize God's purpose in our lives, often stress of deadlines, competing pressures from our sending church versus our receiving church, and our own broken humanity blurs the lines and obscures God's purpose. We are too busy in the moment to accurately evaluate how this situation or interaction with this person fulfills or obstructs God's purpose in our life.

The conclusion of a term or a season of missions is a time of reflection. Here we see things as they might have been. We see why a task was not really that important. A school closes, a clinic is shuttered, a church splits, and we realize that an emphasis on the intangibles would have been far more productive than building buildings. We grieve over hearts wounded in haste. We ask ourselves, "Why didn't we focus more on *being* than on *doing*?" We wonder if our best intentions weren't sabotaged by our best efforts. What of our accomplishments warrants eternal merit?

As a new missionary to Santo, I was told that there was a church half-completed by a former missionary: "Would you please go and finish the building?" Pilon is a beautiful village on the east coast of Santo, at that time a three to four-hour drive, depending on road conditions. Finishing the church required milling out timber, gathering a group of workers, and leading the construction effort. I had never operated a sawmill, learned to speak Bislama, or built anything bigger than a dog house. I was uniquely unsuited for the task.

I sat down on the massive milkwood stump. The ground around me was rocky, strewn with coarse clumps of gray coral. The stump was sticky from the sap oozing out of the fresh cut. The air was hot, still, and filled with the throaty roar of the sawmill engine and the high-pitched whine of its blade cutting through the log twenty feet away. I was tired, nauseous, and as I sat there, waves of fever and chills washed over me. But I stayed. Missionaries don't quit, ever. Right? Unknown to me, I was experiencing the beginnings of what would be a six-month illness that would require multiple surgeries to overcome and nearly cost me my life. Today I was just sick.

Finally Tony, the only church member trained to operate the sawmill, finished the log he was milling, and we headed for home. The road was horrible. Mile after mile, the truck crept over a potholed and rutted path. Burning fever, waves of nausea, tortuous roads, and insistent chatter in a language I did not know drove me to desperation. I longed to get home and rest. But I kept a game face on; I'm the missionary.

At last the road improved enough for me to leave second gear. The young men in the back of the truck whooped and hollered as I approached the unheard-of speed of forty-five miles an hour. Gravel crunched and popped beneath my flying tires; I was going home.

On the right-hand side of the road, I noticed an old man and his dog. The old man was bent and spare, his high cheekbones, strong jawline, boney shoulders, and individual ribs clearly visible. He leaned against his walking stick, a dark-brown bag of bones, sinew, and skin. His dog was a perfect match. It was a deep reddish brown, poor and skinny, every rib and vertebra outlined clearly by its clinging skin. Its boney tail whipped back and forth, and it nudged its owner's hand with its pointed nose. The bond between them was palpable.

Seconds before I passed the old man, his dog stepped into the road and bent to worry a flea near the base of its tail. Options flashed through my mind: I could slam on my brakes, but I knew there was no way I could stop in time. I could swerve to miss the dog, but I visualized young men being thrown from the back as the truck fishtailed on the loose gravel. I made a split-second judgment. The dog would die. The dull thud of the undercarriage hitting the dog was followed by a bump as my rear wheel passed over it.

In my rearview mirror, the dog lay sprawled on the gravel road, and a cloud of dust swirled around the old man. The young men in the truck laughed, and the pastor with me commented, "The dog shouldn't have been in the road." We roared on down the road.

Did I make the right decision? Yes, I couldn't risk the lives of the young men in the back of the truck to save the life of a dog. But why didn't I stop? I was tired, I was sick, and I was on a deadline. Tony had a night job, and I had to get him home on time.

But why didn't I stop? In the moment, going on seemed the right thing to do. I was a busy missionary; I had a job to do, a schedule to keep, and a church building to finish. The old man should have kept his dog out of the road.

In hindsight? I finished the church building, but no pastor was ever willing to serve there. That little building sits vacant Sunday after Sunday, slowly rotting away. Within a month, Tony had left that job for another. What an opportunity I missed. If I had focused on my purpose rather than my task, I could have represented Christ to that old man.

That scene haunts me. A sinewy old man leaning on his cane. An affectionate dog nuzzling his hand. Friends and partners for a long time. The roar of a diesel engine. A swirling cloud of dust. A broken body. An old face lined with grief.

I wonder what he thinks of missionaries and their trucks.

How different things look in conclusion.

Let Justice Roll like a River

The church house was still; only the steady swish of ceiling fans broke the silence, dutifully forcing hot air down on the crowd. The air mingled with the sweat and stale exhaled breath, pushed down past the overheated justices, magistrates, barristers, lawyers, law clerks, and various other members of the Supreme Court of Vanuatu. It swept up the dust lying on the cracked and faded vinyl tiles, moved out toward the cinderblock walls before being sucked up by those same insistent fans to repeat the process.

With each revolution, the heat intensified, the smell of sweat and body odor thickened, and the air became more stifling to breathe. I sat on a folding chair, Bible on my lap, and pitied those before me. They were dressed in costumes designed long ago for cold northern European courtrooms—long flowing black robes, ornamental blouses, heavy ties—and crowned with elaborate wigs. We were gathered for the opening of the 2005 session of the Supreme Court of Vanuatu in Luganville.

Being a missionary in Vanuatu means that sometimes you get to do things you would have never imagined, like opening the court. This is not a matter of praying a ceremonial prayer, carefully worded to avoid offense. No, today is an opportunity to speak God's word into the lives of judges, lawyers, court clerks, the heads of the police and army, members of parliament, custom chiefs, lord mayors of municipalities, and presidents of provinces. The only guideline: "Try and keep it to under an hour."

The quietness is broken as the chief justice steps to the pulpit to read the text I have selected, Micah 6:8: "He hath shewed thee, O man, what is good; and what doth the LORD require of thee, but to do justly, and to love mercy, and to walk humbly with thy God?" (KJV) He finishes, closes the Bible, and returns to his chair, leaving the pulpit vacant. Now it is my time.

I always feel small behind the pulpit but this day especially so. For two millennia, the church has been a force for justice and mercy in this world. The record is not perfect as the church is not composed of perfect people, yet it has been the church that has stood for the oppressed and downtrodden. In Western society, ministers of the gospel led the fight against evils such as slavery and racial discrimination. Here in Vanuatu, it was the church that prevailed against such practices as constant tribal warfare, the strangulation of widows, and cannibalism. Today, in my own small way, I continue that tradition of the church.

I remind the lawyers that true humility means placing great value upon all people, rich and poor, gifted and challenged, men and women. I urge political leaders and officers of the police and army to display mercy as they, as all men, will need the mercy of God. I ask judges and magistrates to be reminiscent that they will in turn be judged by the Creator of heaven and earth, and to be just in all their rulings.

Shortly, I will pray over these judges. I will be asking God to guide their decisions, to guard their integrity, and to draw them into close relationship with himself. For now I close with this quote from Amos 5:24: "But let justice roll on like a river, righteousness like a never-failing stream" (KJV).

Holy Fire

I stoop low to enter the kitchen. As I pull aside the burlap-bag door, a mixture of steam and smoke curls out into the cool evening air. I pause for a moment to take in the scene before me. The dirt floor is pitted and roiled from numerous evacuations for cooking fires. Crosscuts of logs, functioning as stools, are scattered randomly across the floor. Short bamboo walls give way to low-hanging *natanggura* thatched eaves. The network of rafters and battens, the vines used to fasten the thatch to the battens, and the thatch itself are all thickly crusted with black smoke.

Cross members stretch low across the peak of the roof to form a low ceiling and create a storage area for dry firewood. Baskets of foodstuffs and ash-encrusted ears of seed corn hang directly over the cooking fire. Additional supplies of firewood are stacked on the right side of the kitchen. To my left, a pile of sleeping mats provides evidence that the kitchen doubles as a bedroom.

I crouch low to avoid the firewood ceiling and waddle to a foot-high log stool positioned close to the center post. Squatting, I come to rest on my stool, tuck my feet hard up against my bit of log, and lean back onto the hardwood center post. Pastor Peter sits on a bit of log to my right. Once I have settled onto my stool, I scan the room.

Between me and the doorway, an elderly lady squats to tend the fires underneath steaming cast-iron pots. Swirling tendrils of smoke wrap around her, partially obscuring my view. Maybe fifty, she gives proof that life in the bush prematurely ages you. Wide thick feet permanently stained with mud and topped with thick ragged toenails anchor her to the dirt floor just beyond the fire pit. Her grass skirt parts over her knees, revealing infection-scarred calves and thighs. Her bare breasts hang long and flat against her abdomen. Her head and jaw are wrapped tightly in a filthy cloth. One or perhaps several of her teeth are slowly rotting away. Pain clouds her face. What can she do? There are no dentists and no doctors.

Between the elderly lady and me, a young man and his wife sit on the firewood piled against the wall. The young man is dressed in a pair of jogging shorts and a tattered T-shirt. His wife wears a large shirt stretched taut over a pregnant belly and a wraparound skirt tucked neatly around her knees. They both have clear, bright eyes. I know without them telling me that they are the bridge between worlds.

His parents represent the past, a lifestyle barely indistinguishable from that of their ancestors, who have scratched out a living from these muddy hillsides for the last thousand years. This young couple was sent out of the village as children. They have seen the outside world, glimpsed a vastly different life, and received an education. They envision a radically different future for their tribe.

Further in the kitchen, a second fire burns. Its wood is drawn from a separate stack lying against the far wall. There are no pots on this fire. It is configured in the classic Ni-Vanuatu style, with three sticks sticking out like spokes on a wheel. At the hub of the wheel, a small fire smolders. It is marked by a pile of ash, a thin wisp of smoke, a few glowing embers, and a tiny flame. An old man pulls a bit of roasted taro from the ashes, scrapes it clean with a dull knife, and begins to eat.

The old man is the perfect counterbalance to the old woman. Short and thick, he squats next to the fire, his wide flat feet close together, his haunches resting on the back of broad muscular calves, and his knees spread wide. A *nambas*, is pulled tight against his round belly by a vine tied around his waist. The nambas is the entirety of his clothing. His hairless scrotum hangs freely between his thighs. He leans slightly forward, his short muscular arms resting on his knees while his right hand, holding the taro, moves slowly, almost mechanically, back and forth to and from his mouth. Heavy jaws covered with rough gray stubble chew in a circular pattern, and his dark eyes peer out from beneath thick brows.

The old woman digs deep into the first pot and piles plates high with steaming rice. She spoons the soup, a mixture of dark island greens and darker tuna fish, from the second pot and over the rice. The young man hands me the first plate and a large spoon. The plate is visibly dirty; the spoon drips cold water from a dishpan filled with murky water. Bits of rice from the last meal stick to the bowl and handle of the spoon. I push health and hygiene concerns from my mind and, after a short prayer, join the old woman, the young couple, and Pastor Peter in eating the strongly fish-flavored rice.

The old man doesn't join us. He sits alone and isolated, slowly and deliberately eating his taro. He shares the simple hut but not his fire. His fire, the small one at the far end of the kitchen, is a *tabu faea*, or holy flame. His wife and daughter-in-law are forbidden to touch the wood it will burn, the food that will cook on it, or even the scraps of food prepared on it. Only men like him who have been initiated by secret rites can partake of this fire.

The concept of holy fire is not confined to Ni-Vanuatu culture. Moses tells us of a fire that fell from heaven and consumed the first sacrifice at the dedication of the tabernacle. Aaron's sons were struck dead by God for attempting to burn incense with strange fire, or fire that had its origins beyond the flame God himself kindled on the altar.

The Levites were given careful instructions regarding the care of the fire and the necessity of never allowing it to die. During Ahab's turn to Baal worship and persecution of the worshipers of Jehovah, one presumes that the fire on the altar was allowed to die. However, on Mount Carmel, God answered the prayers of Elijah and once more allowed the fire of heaven to consume the sacrifice, rekindling the flame of heaven on Earth.

This is not the first time I have seen old men jealously guarding a tabu fire in Vanuatu. Deep in the Kastom areas of Tanna, Santo, and Pentecost, I have watched aged men go to great lengths to keep an ancient fire burning and free from the corrupting touch of women or the uninitiated. Ask them about its origins, and they answer with mute stares. They hold such knowledge too sacred to share with outsiders.

I am here in this smoky kitchen, eating food I really don't care for, in conditions that I consider seriously unhealthy, because God has once again kindled his holy fire on Earth. His fire fell not on a bloody sacrifice on a stone altar but on 120 men and women that had presented themselves as living sacrifices. That fire ignited on the day of Pentecost has not died out but has been preserved in the hearts of his people for two millennia.

This fire excludes no one: Jew, Gentile, male, female, bond, free—all are welcome to partake. This fire first burned in my heart when I was a six-year-old boy, and it burns still today. It propels me here to this smoky hut to share Christ so that his fire can burn in their hearts as well.

Jonas

The road to the Erakor Church is a mosaic of color. A bright-blue sky is capped with crisp white clouds. Above you, the feathery fronds of coconut palms provide an airy green canopy to shade you from the intense sun. As your eyes follow the thin trunks of the palms down, you note that their bark is stained red, yellow, and orange with moss, and at random intervals, glossy green ferns seem to erupt from their sides. Lower still, the floor of this abandoned plantation is painted by a riotous parade of tropical floral. The canvas is deep green, but scattered throughout are bright yellow orbs of citrus, brilliant reds and purples of bougainvilleas, cheery yellows and oranges of birds-of-paradise, and huge yellow and red hibiscus blossoms. Taro plants spring from the muddy floor, creating huge green tropical umbrellas. Their massive heart-shaped leaves are thick and shiny. Beads of water left over from the morning's rain dot them and glisten like diamonds in the sun.

The road to the Erakor Church makes its way through this brilliant montage. The Bermuda grass that makes up the road is pale green, in contrast to the foliage on either side. Along the length of the road are ruts and mud puddles, their rich brown color adding a pleasing accent to balance the palette of colors surrounding them. Though the road needs no further decoration, this is Sunday. Because it is Sunday, the road is decorated with families making their way to church. The men, dressed in solemn shades and carrying thick, heavy Bibles of deep blue, lead each family and carefully weave their way around the mud. The women and girls follow, clad in brightly colored island dresses edged with a dazzling display of lace and ribbons.

At the end of the road is a simple cement-block building. Inside, a noisy band plays an island version of modern worship songs far too loudly. The interior is rapidly filling with very somber colors in the men's section and a women's section bursting with color. Children run and play on the grassy church lawn, and just outside the door huddles a small group of serious-looking men. This is the pastor, his assistant, and his deacons.

The order of a church service in Vanuatu is often less about leading the saints in worship than about giving each of the assembled pastors and deacons an opportunity to be up front. It is a rather disjointed affair as a different pastor or deacon leads each part of the service. In fact, I am convinced that many parts of the service were invented to give more people the opportunity to lead.

The role of the pastor is to choose who leads each part of the service. Here, in the shade of the porch, the pastor is passing out assignments. Balancing the skill of various deacons with the egos of each is not a simple task. Today his task is complicated by the addition of an elder he cannot ignore, Jonas. The pastor pauses as he looks at Jonas, trying to think what role will best suit him. "Jonas, today you will lead us in prayer for any special needs." Jonas nods his head in agreement.

Jonas is the father of this church. Years ago Jonas, a native of the island of Paama, came to Erakor to work in this plantation. He was disappointed to find that there was no full gospel church nearby, so he would gather his children together each Sunday and, with his guitar in hand, lead them in a simple worship service and teach them the Word. Others began to join them, and from this simple beginning, a church was born. Once it had grown beyond his capacity to lead, a pastor was called, and Jonas moved on.

Jonas, when I first met him, was an old man for a Ni-Vanuatu—at least fifty. He had a cheerful face, was soft-spoken, moved and worked in a slow, deliberate way, and provided some of the finest cement finish work you could find in Santo. Jonas first worked with me when I was building Hope Clinic in Big Bay. I was determined to use only volunteer labor, but Pastor Dick prevailed on me to pay Jonas a small stipend. Over the next few months, I came to respect Jonas and the work that he did. When it came time for me to build a mission house in Santo, I sought him out. "Jonas, I need you," I told him.

I have many memories of Jonas. It was from him that I first learned of the nature of pockets in Vanuatu. "Missionary, if a tool will fit in a man's pocket, it just needs to go home with him," he told me. It was owing to his wise council that I gave a set of hand tools to each of my workers and instructed them that if they lost them, the replacement would be taken from their pay. Each of my workers loved me for the gift, and Jonas, with one bit of advice, saved me hundreds of dollars.

My favorite memories of Jonas are of him and my youngest son, Eli. While we were building our mission house, Eli was just a baby. Every day at lunch, when the other men were resting, Jonas would come looking for Eli. He would carry him around our yard, cooing at him and playing with him. He would show him various plants and birds and patiently teach him their names in the language of Paama. They became the best of friends, with Jonas adopting Eli as his *bubu*, or grandbaby.

As we began to paint the mission house, I noticed that Jonas had an annoying habit: he would randomly paint his name on the walls of the house. I asked him to stop, but he persisted. "Missionary, this is my house too. Years later someone will see my name and know I helped build it." While I appreciated his desire to leave his mark, I had no desire to have my walls decorated with his name, so I assigned a younger worker to go behind him and find all the places he had put his name and paint over them.

As the work was coming to a close, Jonas told me that he would be leaving me before we were done. "I need to go to Erakor and see my grand-kids," he told me. I was sad to see him go but agreed to give him his final pay, and to say thank you, I purchased a toolbox and filled it with every imaginable tool. When I gave it to him, he thanked me and then told me with a twinkle in his eye, "I put my name in one place where you will never find it."

As the service started in Erakor, the building filled to capacity, the band played enthusiastically, the choir sang with passion, the sun beat unmercifully on the tin roof, the temperature began to rise, and sweat began to flow. The pastor, recognizing that there needed to be a change of pace, quieted the band and called for Jonas to lead the church in prayer. Jonas moved to the pulpit in his slow, deliberate way. Standing behind the pulpit, he looked out at the church that had grown from those simple meetings in his home so many years ago. Memories flooded his mind.

In a trembling voice, he said, "Yumi prea. Let us pray." He bowed his head, closed his eyes, and prayed, "Masta blong mi. My Lord."

He was surprised when a clear voice answered "Yes." Jonas opened his eyes and gasped to see Christ face-to-face.

In the church at Erakor, Jonas's children gathered around their father and began to weep as he lay lifeless on the floor.

A few days later, I leaned back on my couch in our newly completed mission house. There, barely visible against the white paint of the ceiling, was one word: *Jonas*.

You Remember That Big Nakavika Tree?

I served at a church in Alabama, so I am used to ambiguous directions. Seemed like every time I asked for directions in Greenville, Alabama, they revolved around the water tower. "You know waer da wata tawer is?" they would ask in a slow Southern drawl. The only problem was that there were four water towers in Greenville. When I asked which water tower, I was given answers of dubious benefit, like "The new one" or "The one behind Peanut's house." Ugh!

Turns out I had no idea what ambiguous directions were till I arrived in Vanuatu. Here directions are almost always based on trees. "Go till you get to the mango," the sweet little widow lady tells me as I take her home after church. I glance up the road ahead and count no fewer than nine mango trees. When I pull to a stop in front of the first mango, she corrects me: "No, missionary, the one close to the banana trees." No self-respecting Ni-Vanuatu family has a yard without banana trees, so this information is only marginally helpful.

Then there is the whole right versus left issue. In most local languages here in Vanuatu—we have over one hundred on the island of Santo alone—there is no equivalent to *right* and *left*. *Right* means the first direction that you turned; *left* is the opposite direction. If you turn right first, then right is *right*, and all is well. However, if you turn left first, then left is *right* and right is *left*, and missionaries get very confused. I will never forget the day I turned right when, unbeknown to me, left was right. "No missionary," Pastor Dick told me with frustration in his voice, "the other right!"

To overcome this frustrating system of right and left, most Ni-Vanuatu prefer to use the terms *down* or *up* to convey direction. This is all well and good in the hills, but on flat land? One day I was gingerly guiding my truck through a swamp well off the beaten track. Paul, my friend and guide for the day, was leading me safely through. We were weaving our way through palm trees and swamp taro when we came to a particularly hairy-looking place. Paul strained to see a safe path. "Go forward, more, more," he urged, and then he realized he had made a mistake and was taking me into a hole. "Quick, missionary, go up there." Since I understood *up there* to mean straight ahead, we were soon hopelessly bogged down.

I learned that day that *up* and *down* refer not to the lay of the land but rather to the direction from the ocean. Up is away from the ocean, down is toward the ocean. Makes perfect sense, except when you cannot *see* the ocean!

Or how about this one: "Just follow the road." I am standing on a goat trail on top of a hill in Big Bay; in front of me are three divergent paths. The sun is going down, and my guide is out of sight in the dense growth in front of me. In response to my shouted query of "Which way?" I am told, "Just follow the road." The term *road* is very fluid here in Vanuatu. It can refer to anything from a paved two-lane road to a barely discernable path through the jungle. Somehow I am supposed to clairvoyantly know which of the three paths in front of me is "the road."

After eight years of dealing with such ambiguous directions, I had to laugh at myself when I found myself on the cell phone telling Pastor Falau, who was lost in the middle of the jungle surrounded by nothing but trees, "You remember that big *nakavika* tree?"

Our new missionary associates were on their way to their new home by themselves for the first time. Their home is three hours from town, and the last hour is on a poorly defined four-wheel-drive trail through the dense jungle. I wanted them to make the trip independent of me, but I didn't want them to be alone, so I sent two pastors, Falau and Taso, with them to push the truck out of the mud if they got stuck, which they did, and to help them find the way if they got lost, which they also did.

I was dressing for church that afternoon when I got the call from Pastor Falau. "Missionary, we seem to have lost the road. I am worried."

"Don't worry," I told him. "You remember that big nakavika tree? When you get to the big nakavika tree where the white man used to live thirty years ago, go down. When you reach the ocean, go to the burao trees and go up. After that, just follow the road; you will be fine!" They were!

Why Do I Have So Much?

I remember clearly my first trek as a missionary to Vanuatu. I, along with Pastor Dick, Missionary Tim Pike, and a handful of others, set out to trek from Talatas to White Grass—as the crow flies, only an eight-mile hike. However, the crumpled terrain requires you to walk closer to twenty-five to complete the trip. We left our wives and children at the coastal village of Matandas. We tooled up the beach in an aluminum skiff till we reached the stone-covered beach at Talatas. Eagerly we scrambled up the steep beach, shouldered our backpacks, and set out on an adventure. I had no idea what was coming.

The first couple of miles transitioned us from ocean-side scrub to the wide-open understory of a coconut plantation and then into what I considered at the time dense jungle. We jumped small streams, bantered cheerfully, and took lots of pictures. At the village of Wosayolo, we met with church members and picked up our guide for the trip. At the time, I casually examined the half-finished clinic building, having no concept how big a role this place would play in my future ministry.

Samuel, our young guide, led us out of Wosayolo and straight into the swamp. Soon the trek became less fun. We waded through waist-deep pools and stumbled out onto mud banks where we sank knee-deep into thick gooey mud. We linked up arm in arm to cross rain-swollen rivers and paused on their banks to pick the leeches off our calves. We left the soggy floodplain and began to climb ridiculously steep hillsides. Pastor Dick cut hand- and toeholds into the slippery clay with his bush knife and traversed up and down the steep hillsides, assisting each member of the team.

As we walked, we were pummeled by heavy rains. The hillsides became more treacherous. The group moved slower. Samuel became impatient and repeatedly warned us that if we didn't move faster, we would be caught in the jungle by the coming darkness. In my wisdom as a new missionary, I was wearing blue jeans and tennis shoes. The water and mud caked on my jeans and shoes till moving my legs was an exercise in weight lifting. I lingered for a moment on the side of a particularly steep hill and questioned God as to why he had called the bookworm to Vanuatu, instead of my athletic classmates in Bible School.

Night fell, and we had failed to reach the village. Pitch darkness descended on the rain forest. Thick clouds blocked out the last of the sun's rays and the rising moon. Rain, heavy sheets of rain fell, further obstructing our view. Samuel, exasperated at our slow progress, abandoned us on the path and took shelter in a lone house that stood at the top of the hill. Our calls for direction were met with an insistent "Just follow the path!"

That night we slept on the dirt floor of a tiny thatch hut. The next day we completed the journey. My clothes were filthy. Every muscle in my body screamed with pain, but I had made it. For the next couple of days, we lived in the *nakamal* at White Grass. We slept on stiff bamboo platforms without the aid of mattresses or blankets. We relieved ourselves in a flooded outhouse. We ate food cooked over a smoky fire.

I was living my dream. The scene in the long low nakamal was straight out of a *National Geographic*. The dirt-floored, thatch-roofed building was shared by several families. The men and boys wore only loincloths, and the women and girls wore only a few leaves draped from a vine tied around their waists. The bushmen welcomed me to their fire, and I sat up late each night, drinking steaming cups of orange leaf tea, tasting taro and *lap lap* for the first time, and trying to make out enough of the language to engage in the dialogue. I had arrived!

A young chief by the name of Norman befriended me. He had been raised in town and received an education, so he spoke good but accented English. He introduced me to his family, patiently explained the system of fires in the nakamal, the role of the chief, and answered all my other questions. We traded stories each night, and his wife, Salome, cooked for us. To this day, I consider Salome the best cook in Vanuatu. Since my arrival in Vanuatu, I had been surrounded by pastors and church leaders. In Norman I had found my first nonpastor Ni-Vanuatu friend.

Too soon, in my opinion, it was time for us to head back down the mountainside. Chief Norman led us back to Talatas. The weather was kinder, and the path was much easier to travel going downhill. Still, the weight of my jeans exhausted my legs, and I found myself stumbling by the time we made it to the beach at Talatas. We landed at Matandas to the cheers of our children, tired, hungry for Western food, but quite happy with our trip.

We all packed into my waiting truck and sped off to town. Back at our house, we showered, luxuriating in the hot water, changed into clean clothing, and headed to the local pizza restaurant for our fix of Western food. The evening passed quickly as Tim and I regaled our wives with tales of our adventures.

That night I stepped into my clean, tile-floored, air-conditioned bedroom and sank into my soft bed. Then it hit me; it felt like a physical blow. My new friends were huddled around a smoky fire, eating bland, tasteless food, preparing to sleep on the floor or a hard bamboo platform. I found myself struggling with the inequity of our lives. Why should I have so much and they so little?

Fast-forward fourteen years. Another Ni-Vanuatu friend has just returned to Vanuatu from a six-month work visa to New Zealand and joined my work crew at Sanma Bible Training Center. As we drove home from the work site one day, we chatted about his time in New Zealand. We talked about all the wonderful, inexpensive food. We swapped stories of fishing for New Zealand's giant rainbow trout. As we battled the hot, humid air, we talked about snow, skiing, fireplaces, and cold winter nights.

My friend had just experienced a Western standard of living. He had drawn Western wages and enjoyed the low prices for food and goods that come from free trade. Yet here he was, bouncing along in my truck over abominable third-world roads. He just finished a hard day's work, just as hard as what he had done in New Zealand, and for this day's work, he had drawn the same pay as he had received for working one hour in New

Zealand. Again I found myself faced with the perplexing question: Why should I have so much and they so little?

As far as poverty is concerned, Vanuatu is a wonderful place to be poor. There is plenty of food for everyone. All the materials you need to build a house are readily available in the environment. The weather is mild enough that you really can live your entire life without clothing and never need fear becoming ill from exposure to the elements. While many of my friends have no cash and don't have access to the things cash can buy, in reality they don't suffer physical want like the poor in other countries. Yet it doesn't resolve the question: Why should I have so much and they so little?

There is nothing inherent about being an American or a Westerner that makes a person or his or her time more valuable. The short answer is, there is no reason I should have more and they less. But it is also true that there is no reason they should have more and I less. As strange as it may sound, there is no reason why we should all have equal shares. There is nothing unjust about an unequal distribution of wealth.

Wealth is amoral. It can be used for good or evil. The morality or lack thereof is in the possessor of wealth, not the wealth itself. Wealth is not synonymous with happiness. Wealth has little to no impact on one's ability to live a meaningful life.

To those without God, there seems to be an arbitrary randomness to the distribution of wealth around the world. Ron Crocombe in *The South Pacific* insists that this unequal distribution of wealth springs from "the accident of birth." Jared Diamond in *Guns, Germs, and Steel* goes to great lengths to explore the environmental, sociological, and cultural factors that contribute to the global inequality of wealth.

I feel uncomfortable with my undeserved larger share of wealth than my friends. However, other than choosing an ascetic lifestyle so that I share in their poverty, there is little I can do to change it. Try as I might, I can't raise the economic level of an entire country. Living in Vanuatu forces me to confront a world of economic inequality. But this is not just about me. The truth is that in a global context, all but the most abjectly poor Westerners are incredibly wealthy.

While those without God focus on the arbitrariness of wealth distribution, Christians should focus on the responsibility that comes with greater wealth. Christ taught that "Everyone to whom much was given, of him much will be required" (Luke 12:48, [ESV]). Each one of us will answer not for the relative imbalance of wealth but for what we did with the wealth we possessed.

The more pressing question is, "Once I am aware of this global imbalance, how do I live out the Golden Rule?" If I were the poor, how would I want the rich to use their wealth? In the story of the Good Samaritan, Jesus taught us that our *neighbors* are not defined by ethnic, national, or religious identity. Instead, your *neighbor* is anyone you see in need.

Seventeen years as a missionary and I still struggle daily with living out the Golden Rule in a context where I am wealthier than the majority of my neighbors. I don't claim to have the answers, but knowing that dignity matters more than money, I vow to respond with love to the needs I see, respect the humanity of every individual, value and respect the culture of my neighbors, refuse to assign status based on wealth, and refuse to relate to my neighbors based on their usefulness to me or my cause.

Why do I have so much? Clearly, because God wants me to do so much. Why do you have so much?

Magic Jesus

The pastor climbed down from the truck slowly. Age and size forced him to move slowly. His short frame was stooped with years, his hair was gray, and his face was round and friendly, easy to trust. He was a large man; too many years eating too much food had taken its toll. Swollen feet shuffled to find their place in his sandals before he set out for the house before him. He wore baggy brown pants, a road-wrinkled white shirt, and a tattered cardigan sweater that seemed terribly out of place in the tropical heat.

The house before him was really no more than a hut. The dirt floor was covered with mats. The walls were a single ply of woven bamboo. The frame of the house was poles from the local forest. Its roof was a thatch of sago palm leaves. It contained no kitchen, no plumbing, and no privacy. It was a place to sleep at night and a place to hide from the rain. Yet it was home for a troubled family.

Months ago the mother of this family had first noticed the lump in her breast. Sure that it was a temporary anomaly, she ignored it. However, it had proven to be anything other than temporary; instead of dissipating, it grew and spread. At night, as her family slept, she lay awake under the sago palm thatch, her heart racing, her throat tight with fear—sure now of her own diagnosis, terrified of its consequences. In Vanuatu, breast cancer is a death sentence: not a quick painless death but a horrifying drawn-out torture with only Tylenol to ease the pain. Every woman has witnessed the agonizing death of another from breast cancer. No one eases into the night with morphine-aided rest here.

Weeks ago she had broken down and told her husband the news. They wept in stunned silence in the privacy of their little hut. No one needed to tell them the futility of seeking medical help. Still, in a desperate bid to save his wife, the husband insisted they visit the local hospital. Maybe she was wrong; maybe it was something else, something curable. Desperate for hope, they made the two-hour trip to town only to have their hope cruelly dashed. With tears of compassion, the nurses advised her to return home to die.

In Vanuatu, nothing just happens. Underpinning the Melanesian world view is the idea that everything—life, death, sickness, health, good grades on school exams, bad grades on school exams, mechanical breakdowns, and accidents—are all caused. Children don't fail their tests because they didn't study; no, children fail their tests because the parents of competing students paid a witch doctor to hex them. An accident on a work site doesn't happen because someone slipped on a ladder; it was caused by a mischievous spirit toying with the workers. The causes of disaster in Vanuatu can range from curses placed by witch doctors to angry words polluting the ground. Finding the cause is deemed to be essential to finding the cure.

Melanesians believe that there is a life-force that flows through everything. It is not so much that they believe that inanimate objects are alive in and of themselves but rather that life flows through them. Certain objects, words, and places are believed to form powerful vortexes or to serve as lenses that can focus this life-force. Manipulated properly, these objects and words can affect the physical environment. They can bring or stop rain, wind, earthquakes, and hurricanes. They can cause or heal sickness, bring prosperity or want. Some men are known to be especially perceptive to spiritual issues. It is believed that they can sense these disturbances that happen in the flow of the life-force that pervades our environment, find the cause, and cure it.

The old pastor shuffles his way to the humble hut. There are no pleasantries exchanged. The pastor's face is stoic, as if he is saving all his energy for the task ahead. An underling explains to the family that they will have to leave the house for the pastor to make a thorough search. The family and the underling make their way to the shade of a massive banyan tree just off the beach. They sit there in the green grass, cooled by the ocean breeze, and make small talk, the family pretending that their whole life isn't tied up in what the pastor is doing in the house.

Heavy on the husband's thoughts is the cost of today. To hire someone such as the pastor for a minor issue like school exams or a pesky cough is simple, requiring only a few days' work. However, cancer is the costliest thing to cure, with the price tag often being thousands of dollars. Even with borrowing from family, he will be left with a substantial debt. Is it worth it? Of course! He loves his wife, and the pastor has a solid reputation, with many clients vouching for the veracity of his cures. The pastor has a magic Jesus.

Unfortunately, in Vanuatu, belief in a magic Jesus is all too common. It finds its roots in the Melanesian belief that words too can serve as a vortex for the underlying life-force. These words are most commonly ancestral names. Far too many in Vanuatu have failed to understand that Jesus Christ is a risen Savior, that he lives with us today, that he bodily sits at the right hand of the Father, and that soon he himself will be returning to carry his bride away. To many, "Jesus" is merely another ancestral name, another arrow in the quiver of spiritually perceptive and gifted men.

With their minds heavy in thought, no one notices the little one slip away. He is curious. "What is that pastor doing in our house?" he wonders. Quietly he makes his way to the back of the hut and peeks through the open window. Inside the darkness of the hut, the pastor mutters to himself, moving from room to room. I wonder, what is going through his mind? What made him pursue this path? Did he ever truly know Christ? Does he honestly believe his own propaganda?

To the little one's amazement, the pastor pulls a small fetish from his pocket and deposits it under the mother's bed before turning for the front door. Once at the door, the pastor calls for the mother and father. Sadly he leads them to bed and shows them the fetish underneath it.

Shaking his head, he tells them it is the work of a powerful witch doctor. The couple is horrified and elated—horrified because this means they have a determined enemy, elated because once the curse is removed, a cure is surely possible. More money changes hands, and the pastor performs a purification ceremony. A grateful family ushers him back to the truck.

As the truck prepares to leave, the little one whispers to his father what he has witnessed. The father turns purple with rage and confronts the pastor. The pastor's denials are not convincing enough, and the father pummels the pastor.

That night, silence reigns in the little hut. Once again fear chokes them. Their faith has been crushed. Now they have no hope. There is no magic Jesus.

Author's note: Tragically, this is a true story. The pastor really does claim to have a magic Jesus, the little boy really did witness his deception, and the father really did pummel the pastor. The mother really did die an agonizing death. The great tragedy is that the deception of this pastor increased the resistance to the gospel in this community. Pray God will give honest ministers of the gospel in Vanuatu.

Oceans

How do you describe the ocean? It's broad and flat and deep. It's narrow and shallow and covered with shifting mountains. It's still and quiet and peaceful. It's torn by rapid tides and it roars and fills you with terror. It's blue and sparkling and friendly. It's gray and dark and moody.

How do you describe the ocean? An implacable mistress with ever-shifting moods. A gentle lover that cradles all who surrender to its embrace. An abundant provider of rich food, forgotten treasure, and benevolent weather. A thief that entices you with deceptive calm, robs you of your breakfast, and then steals all that is precious and dear.

How do you describe the ocean? It blazes a brilliant white at sunrise. It radiates brilliant blues and greens under the midday sun. It ripples and shimmers like a sequined dress on a beautiful woman. It sulks with bland grays when shadowed by clouds. It burns deep amber at the setting sun.

How do you describe the ocean? It dances with silvery accents under the moonglow. It's an oily black film rising and falling on cloud-covered nights. It's a million diamonds sparkling under the stars. It's brilliant sparks of green phosphorus at the stroke of a paddle's caress.

How do you describe the ocean? It lies still and quiet in the hot days of summer. It springs to life under playful breezes. It screams in fury at the approaching storm. It quiets itself under the gentle touch of the rain.

How do you describe the ocean? It brings warmth to cold, barren islands. It provides cooling relief to sunburned bathers. It births whispering sea breezes through coconut palms. It yields refreshing rain to parched islands. It spawns murderous cyclones.

How do you describe the ocean? It lays glassy calm before your boat. It splinters into a million perfect orbs that sparkle with the brilliance of diamonds in the sunlight. It supports you with a firm grasp, keeping you from falling into the abyss below. It pushes restlessly against your forward movement, protesting each foot of progress. It closes seamlessly after your passing, erasing all record of your presence.

How do you describe the ocean? It swaddles a thousand islands in a tender embrace. It softly caresses delicate white beaches. It playfully rearranges pebble and stone landings. It patiently digs away at clay banks. It crashes with fury against unmoving stones. It tunnels under cliff faces, eating deep into the hidden earth.

How do you describe the ocean? It sings a lullaby to the exhausted with gentle swishes. It whispers love songs to the romantic with lazy ripples. It throws howling taunts at the storm tossed with rude surf. It calls to its playmates with the hollow thump of breakers on the beach.

How do you describe the ocean? It shamelessly pursues the sun and moon. It slips out of harbors in the dead of night. It abandons thousands of pools teeming with life along its shores. It returns with an impatient surge. It floods over stony reefs. It strains to exceed its bounds. It slips away again.

Mountain Shower

It has been a hot, sweaty day digging footings, bending rebar, beginning construction on a new church. I am covered with dirt and grime and seriously looking forward to a shower. The shower facilities, when I inspected them earlier, looked rustic but adequate: four walls, a real door, a pebble floor, and best of all, running water.

After we put away our tools and discuss the next day's work, I begin to make my way up the hill to my room and shower. The road up to the lodge is rutted but wide, the incline gentle enough to climb without getting too out of breath. I am shocked to see other members of our team coming down to meet me, carrying their towels and soap. I guess the consternation and confusion on my face is significant enough inquiry. "No water," they tell me. "We are going to swim in a pool. Go grab your towel."

I know all about pools in Vanuatu. First of all, they are never as close as promised. A pool that is a five-minute walk away will require at least a half hour of hard hiking. Second, these pools are not the pristine mountain springs you might imagine. Often you must shoo the pigs and cows out before you can luxuriate in the scum-covered water, picking leeches off your ankles while dodging clumps of fecal matter. Been there, done that, got the T-shirt. No, thank you. No pool for me.

We talk with some of the local men, asking where we can find clean water. I place the emphasis on *clean* so that they know I am serious about avoiding the pool. A lively discussion erupts, all in the local village language, leaving me clueless as to what is being said. An old man with wild hair and a bushy beard puffs hard on his pipe before gesturing off to the west. A young man points to a path that leads further down the hill and to the east. Merits are argued, problems are weighed, and a decision is reached. "Get your towel, missionary. We will take you to good water."

I grab my towel and put on swimming shorts and a T-shirt. I slip my soap and shampoo into my pockets, drape my towel over my shoulders, and head off down the path. At first we head down and to the east as if we are headed to the location that the young man had argued for. However, when we reach the bottom of the hill, we head back toward the west and plunge into the thick brush. As we walk, our party grows; giggling children materialize from all quarters. Their presence adds a festive atmosphere to the jaunt, though I am a bit concerned as to why this is an adventure to them.

The problem with the jungle is that you cannot see what is ahead of you; the beauty of the jungle is that you cannot see what is ahead of you. Suddenly the ground rises in front of me; I crane my head back and gaze above me, where a narrow path zigzags back and forth up an impossible hillside before disappearing into the trees. I groan. I have been here before—maybe not this path, maybe not this village, but in this situation. "Where is the water?" I ask my nine-year-old escorts. "On top," they reply before scrambling up the trail.

Nothing is more humiliating than climbing the side of a mountain with nine-year-olds. When you are gasping for breath, they are chattering and singing at the top of their lungs; when you are clinging to precarious hand- and toeholds, asking God to spare you from a painful death, they scamper past you like mountain goats. When you reach an impossible spot, they scramble up the sheer cliff face above you and offer you a hand. They were born and bred on these hills. I am from the flatlands of Texas.

Finally the end comes into sight. Thirty minutes after we began our ascent, thatch houses peek out over the hillside, giving hope that this climb is nearly over. My entourage bursts over the top of the hill, and stunned villagers stare in surprise. They heard the children coming. What they didn't anticipate was the white man. I am too short of breath for much in the way of conversation, but I do manage to get out a simple request to bathe in their water. They smile and point me to the shower.

The shower in this instance is pipe hung about six feet in the air, with a tap. A large block of wood has been placed under it to provide mud-free footing. That is it. No walls, no door, no privacy. Now I understand why the whole trip was an adventure to my guides. They are *really* going to get to see a white man. They are joined by the children of the village and form a circle around the shower. Some lean on trees, others squat, all stare, watching my every move.

I retain my swimming trunks, take off my shirt, and throw it and my towel over a nearby branch. I place my shoes just out of splash range, step under the tap, and start an ice-cold mountain shower. As I bathe, the children chatter excitedly in the local language. Some point to various parts of my anatomy as they jabber away. Peals of laughter ring out. The water is too cold for me to truly enjoy my shower. But one thing is for sure: my guides did.

Water of Life

Twin curses assail the youth of Vanuatu: Bob Marley and yachters. Everywhere you look in Vanuatu, you see evidence of Bob Marley's popularity here; his posters adorn shop windows, T-shirts bear his image, young men cultivate dreadlocks in an attempt to look like him, and his marijuana-promoting music blares from countless loud speakers. Bob Marley cultivates the appetite for marijuana; the yachters provide the seeds and growing advice.

For many young men, marijuana not only provides a numbing relief from the pain of a limited future of island life but also creates the first real economic opportunity they have ever had. A young man living in a village on an isolated island has no hope of a job and almost no means of creating a meaningful income. In a culture where you must purchase your bride, having a bleak fiscal future means having a very bleak physical future as well. However, the same young man has plenty of garden space, is faced with a rapidly expanding demand for pot in the cities, access to daily flights to the capital city, and operates in an environment with virtually no law enforcement. Maybe that explains how a pastor's son became one of Tanna's leading drug dealers.

It is Sunday morning, and we are waiting for everyone to arrive before beginning service. In Vanuatu the service time doesn't determine when people arrive; rather, when people arrive determines the service time. I am sitting on my bamboo bench under the mango that has become my office for the week, munching on a piece of bread and slowly sipping a cup of coffee. A steady stream of pickup trucks rolls into the churchyard, disgorging passengers in its wake. Each truck carries over twenty people. It is going to be quite the crowd this morning. Young men are busy extending the church building with tarps, and old men are building makeshift benches with spare boards, bamboo, and logs.

The church building is simple. The floor is cement and uncluttered by benches or chairs. The cement-block walls are only four feet high, giving the church an open, airy feel with lots of breeze and a clear view of the surrounding yard. The roof is secondhand roofing iron with bright specks of lights peeking through old nail holes. There is no ceiling, so the iron radiates heat like the sides of a wood-burning stove.

Church starts when the building is full. Pastors from around Tanna fill the benches around the perimeter of the building, and women and children pack in cheek to jowl on the floor, sitting on mats of woven pandanas leaves. The pastors have agreed to try a novel way of church today. Normally the service is broken into an infinite number of parts so that each pastor can have his five minutes of fame, with the leader being very sensitive so that none of them feel slighted. Today there will be only one pastor leading the service, and he is trying instead to be sensitive to the Holy Spirit.

By the time the preaching starts, the crowd has exceeded the building's capacity and spread out over the churchyard. Mothers of preschoolers and nursing babies cluster in the shade of the orange trees. Men and boys are draped over all the remaining trees and any logs available. No electricity means no PA system, so I fill my lungs to the max and do my best to project over the cries of infants, hoping my voice will carry throughout the churchyard. I take my text from Ezekiel 47 and talk about the miracle of the river of life, how it brings life to everything it touches.

As I close my sermon, I observe that in verse 11, we are shown that at every place where the flow of the river was restricted, death remained. As graphically as I can, I describe what death looks like for the body, in a person's spiritual life, in a marriage, and in the church. Then I turn to the words of Christ: "If any man thirst, let him come unto me, and drink. He that believeth on me, as the scripture hath said, out of his belly shall flow rivers of living water."

"Christ still calls the thirsty, he still calls the dying," I tell them. "If you are thirsty, come."

I bow my head to pray; my words can never compel men to come to Christ, but his Spirit can. I pray for the Holy Spirit to do his work. When I look up, the altars are filled. Old men, young men, women, and children are crowded around the front of the church. Bill, the drug dealer, is among them. The son of a Ni-Vanuatu pastor and a Fijian mother, he is a giant among the people of Tanna. Over six feet tall, he towers above all his friends. Today he is kneeling, weeping in the altar. A local pastor kneels with him, his arm around Bill's sob-shaken shoulders, leading him in prayer.

That afternoon, Bill returned to his home and, without any coaching or prodding, uprooted all of his marijuana plants. He spent the next week following me as I ministered in Tanna. Each morning and night, we had devotions together, slowly working our way through the first few chapters of Romans. It was thrilling to see the hunger for God's word in his life. The last morning we had together before I returned to Santo, I had the privilege of baptizing Bill.

I listened as Bill shared his testimony of growing up in church, of pretending in the altar but never finding Christ. He told of finding in marijuana a means of numbing the pain of an empty life. He described the irrational anger he felt anytime he was not stoned. He testified that there at the altar, as he was broken before God, his longing for marijuana was removed, and his heart filled with joy and the peace of God. He paused for a moment as he struggled for words to describe the genuine nature of his experience, finally he said, "My tears felt hot on my face."

If you enjoyed *The Sons of Cannibals* read on for a preview of

Hungry Devils and Other Tales from Vanuatu
By Bryan Webb

Vanuatu

Vanuatu is the land that I love, my surrogate home, the land of my calling.

Vanuatu is misty mountains cloaked with lush tropical rainforests dotted with quaint thatch villages next to cold bubbling springs.

Vanuatu is cascading waterfalls leaping into picturesque alpine valleys that host dancing rivers which spill onto sugar white beaches before emptying into cobalt blue bays.

Vanuatu is the roaring surf churned frothy white on the teeth of coral reefs and windswept ash plains beneath intimidating volcanoes.

Vanuatu is high broken mountains towering over low coral atolls, luxury high-rise condos sitting opposite rust-eaten tin shanties, hand-carved canoes gliding beneath the shadow of million-dollar yachts.

Vanuatu is crimson sunsets that ignite pebble beaches and make white sands glow pink, coastlines lined with a silver thread of moonlight.

Vanuatu is bright eyes, warm smiles, and open hearts.

Vanuatu is the crash of waves, the rumble of volcanoes, the rattle of earthquakes.

Vanuatu is the toll of church bells, the sound of choirs, women's chatter and children's laughter.

Vanuatu is tribal drums beating in the night, the eerie echo of conch shell horns across high mountain valleys, the roar of tropical downpours smashing onto the dense rainforest canopy.

Vanuatu is an old man in a suit and tie laboring over a pulpit in the tropical heat calling men to follow an eternal God.

Vanuatu is young men in penis sheaths springing from elevated towers with vines tied around their ankles, attempting to appease an ancient god with a symbolic sacrifice.

Vanuatu is glittering black volcanic ash, massive spreading banyan trees, brilliantly colored grass skirts swaying the forest reverberating with ancient chants, a ring of dancers springing into the air, coiling their legs and collectively slamming wide bare feet into the *nasara,* or dancing ground. The ground trembling, crashing rain falls like a blanket across the valley, cutting off the outside world, the rest of the island, the rest of the valley, until time has stopped and all there is is here and now. This is Vanuatu.

Vanuatu is an unnumbered myriad of islands, 120 distinct languages, swarthy swaggering six-foot men from Paama, wiry pigmies from Espiritu Santo, blond children with violet eyes on the island of Ra.

Vanuatu is a Christian nation with a living memory of cannibalism. Its coastal communities have served Christ for two centuries while mountain tribes still sit in darkness.

Vanuatu is proud pagan chiefs, subjugated women, malnourished children.

Vanuatu is pre-Christian villagers blinded by the god of this world, enslaved by sin, fearful of unseen spirits, captive to the twin tyrants of ignorance and illiteracy.

Vanuatu is an unlimited opportunity. In the midst of this crushing darkness, if we go, if we preach, some will hear, some will believe, some will call on his name and be saved. We can change eternity with our actions.

Holy Ground

The mud beneath my feet is oozing black and flecked with bits of brown stone. I am standing beneath an enormous bougainvillea bush; its lower branches have been consistently pruned so that it forms a spreading canopy about seven feet above the ground. Grey wisps of cloud seep through the tangle of branches that form this shelter, leaving behind a heavy dew that falls in large cold drops down the collar of my shirt. This is the community of Ponmuili.

Ponmuili is a group of outlying houses from the village of Lonlipli; it sits high on a narrow ridge dividing two valleys on south-central Pentecost Island. It is the site of a two-day clinic with doctors and dentists from Health Care Ministries. Its primary advantage over other prospective sites is that it lies along the only road bisecting the island. We are here because the villages of the Sa people in this area of Pentecost are *kustom*: they have thus far rejected the gospel. They have no churches. Our hope is that as the villagers see the love of Christ displayed, they will want to come to know him.

Before me is a small, low-slung thatch house. Its newly constructed thatch roof and bamboo walls are still fresh and green, waiting to age to a mellow honey color over time. Its dark interior has a mud floor and is divided by curtains into a number of exam rooms. Here doctors and nurses will treat numerous diseases, stitch up victims of domestic abuse, and pass out loads of worming medicine.

Curious villagers are beginning to gather around us. I don't know if they're drawn by the promise of free medical care or if they're just inquisitive about the white folks. Topless women and girls wearing heavy grass skirts gather in shy, giggly clusters, hiding behind one another but watching everything with bright wide eyes. Little boys with palm fronds wrapped around their penises run and jump in the mud, generally enjoying the excitement of foreign visitors to their village. The men proudly wearing only their *numbas* (a bit of woven mat wrapped around the penis) squat in the mud on wide, thick-soled feet. A few of the men smoke cigarettes of dark homegrown tobacco. Their eyes stare without inhibition at the pale, fully clothed visitors while they share witty observations in the Sa language.

At the door of the clinic, Kathleen Ewing, the team leader, is setting up a makeshift pharmacy. Suitcases full of various medicines and assorted supplies are opened to form temporary shelves. A crude table of rough-hewn boards is set up as her working area. A half wall of bamboo serves to keep the crowd at a manageable distance and prevent pilfering. With her curly white hair and gentle smile, she projects a patient grandmotherly image that suggests she would love to spoil you rotten. In truth, Kathleen, a neonatal intensive care nurse from the States, is a no-nonsense leader with years of experience in leading medical teams on short trips to the Pacific islands.

We—missionary families, two dentists, a doctor, a physician's assistant, and four nurses—gather around the pharmacy, trying to escape the constant dripping. Kathleen gives last minute instructions to the team and answers questions. She assigns exam rooms and charges nurses with the responsibility of either triage or dressing, and I pair the medical personnel with various missionaries who serve as translators and introduce our two native Sa translators. The full mission team is fluent in Bislama, the national language, but we expect to see some patients that speak only Sa.

Kathleen asks me to open the clinic with prayer. After my prayer, she leads the team in song. "We are standing on holy ground, and I know that there are angels all around...." I glance at the clinic building with its dark, dirty interior and look down at the mud encasing my feet, noticing the flecks of brown stone glistening in the all-pervasive moisture. *This is holy ground?* I ask myself.

Traditionally, much of the ground in Vanuatu is considered holy. Ni-Vanuatu deem active volcanoes especially holy, and they hold extinct craters in reverence. One such crater on Tanna is named Itapu, literally meaning "this is the holy place," and a valley there is called Enmantange, or "holy ground." For major construction projects, a cultural survey is required before site preparation can begin. Tabu sites, or holy places, must be marked and preserved.

Christians have holy places as well—Calvary, Gesthemeni, Bethlehem, and Mount Sinai. Ground made sacred by God meeting with man. Individuals often view the site of their own salvation with special reverence. But this, this muddy village in the middle of a forgotten island?

Ground is holy where God meets with man. This muddy house may not be Mount Sinai; however, by the Holy Spirit, God gathered this team of medical professionals here. He led Steve and Kara Jeager as they performed the initial survey. He guided our decision to determine the clinic site. He brought us here together from across the United States, led us to the far side of the globe for one purpose—to meet with the Sa people.

Tears run down my cheeks as I realize that here on this muddy mountainside, God is using us to reveal him. This is holy ground!

Note: Before the outreach was finished, more than five hundred patients had been treated, and over half that number met with God for the first time.

The Price of a Pig

I am sitting on two enormous bamboo logs that have been fashioned into a bench of sorts under the shade of a small mango tree. A steady drizzle fills the air, but I am reasonably dry under the canopy. On my lap, I am balancing a plate of Tanna soup, everything that is available thrown into a pot and cooked until tender. Today the soup includes a small pig. With both hands I hold a pork rib and gnaw the meat while attempting to avoid the hairy skin. This is the first meat I have had all week.

The chief catches me in this inconvenient position. I can't stand because of the bowl of soup, I can't shake hands because mine are full of pork ribs, and I can't talk as I have a mouth full of chewy meat. So I do the classic Ni-Vanuatu greeting—I grunt and wiggle my eyebrows. Sort of a nonverbal, "Nice to see you. How are you?" The chief smiles. "Are you enjoying the pig?" he asks. He waits for me to wiggle my eyebrows in the affirmative before continuing. "You see the lady standing by the table? She brought you this pig. In exchange for the pig, she wants you to tell her the truth about God."

Standing at the end of the table is a short plump lady with a shy smile on her face. I would guess that she is in her early fifties. Here in the bush of Tanna, for a woman to approach a man, especially an important guest such as a missionary, is very difficult. Here the men surround me, and I see the women only as they hurry back and forth from the kitchen with pots of food or dishes, always stooped in an exaggerated show of submission and respect and carefully avoiding any eye contact. But by giving a pig, she has obligated me to talk with her.

I am in south Tanna for a pastor's retreat. This church is one of only two Assembly of God churches in its language group. This language group has over seventy villages, a population of over nine thousand, and only seven churches of any kind, which have a total of less than four hundred members. Most of the villages surrounding us are *kustom*, meaning that they follow the traditional animistic Ni-Vanuatu religions. Even in the villages with a church, only a fraction of the population will ever attend. A priority for me is seeing new churches planted in this area.

I nod my head toward the lady, and she approaches timidly. She sits beside me with her eyes fixed on the ground and speaks in such a low voice that I have difficulty hearing her words.

"Missionary," she says, "I need to know the truth." She tells me she is illiterate, making it impossible for her to read the Bible and discover the truth for herself.

She says that she sent one of her boys to the Catholic school and another to the Assembly of God school.

"Why would you do that?" I ask.

"I thought to myself," she says, "that at least one of them will find the road to life." She tells me of visiting priests, teenage Mormon missionaries, and Baha'i teachers that have passed her way, all telling a different version of truth.

"But yesterday, when you spoke, I felt something I had never felt before, so I brought you a pig so that I could ask you to tell me the truth about God."

How sad to have lived a life in the fog of illiteracy. How tragic that the gospels she had received had been conflicting doctrines that further obscured the truth. How desperate the search for truth that would have you commit your children to conflicting views of God in hopes that at least one would be saved. I began with creation and slowly wove the story of God's plan of redemption. I had no way of knowing what she knew or didn't know about God so I assumed nothing and covered everything.

She nods as I tell the story, gradually becoming less timid and more open, even stealing the occasional glance at my face and daring to make eye contact. We talk for over an hour, with me explaining the scriptures. When I ask if she wants to pray and accept Christ as her savior, she says yes, and there under the mango, I lead her in a sinner's prayer. When we finish, her face beams with joy. She found what she came for; she thanks me profusely and repeatedly.

I think back to the day I found Christ as my savior. I too was illiterate. I too knew next to nothing of God. I understood only that I was a sinner, that Christ was a savior, and that if I asked him to, he would take my sins away. That evening at the altar, Christ did just that in fact, he did more— he gave me new life. Over time, I grew and learned to read. I received constant teaching and was able to verify in the Bible what I had been taught. However, my new friend would most likely never have that privilege.

The tragedy of illiteracy strikes me hard as we finish our talk. I wonder how much of our conversation she will retain. I wonder if someone with a smooth tongue will come by at a later date peddling yet another gospel. I wonder how much of God's plan she will ever truly understand.

"Hold to this," I tell her. "Hold to this and never let go—it is through faith in Jesus Christ alone that we have peace with God." With these words, I give her the essence of the gospel. I had to; that was the price of the pig.

Made in the USA
Columbia, SC
20 March 2019